MATH Trailblazers®

A BALANCED MATHEMATICS PROGRAM INTEGRATING SCIENCE AND LANGUAGE ARTS

Unit Resource Guide
Unit 11
Looking at 100

THIRD EDITION

KENDALL/HUNT PUBLISHING COMPANY
4050 Westmark Drive   Dubuque, Iowa 52002

A TIMS® Curriculum
University of Illinois at Chicago

UIC The University of Illinois
at Chicago

The original edition was based on work supported by the National Science Foundation under grant
No. MDR 9050226 and the University of Illinois at Chicago. Any opinions, findings, and conclusions
or recommendations expressed in this publication are those of the author(s) and do not necessarily
reflect the views of the granting agencies.

Letter Home

Looking at 100

Date: _____

Dear Family Member:

In this unit, we focus on the number 100 as we explore number relationships in a variety of contexts.

Your child will use different manipulatives to "see" the number 100 and to solve addition and subtraction problems. For example, your child will group and count coins and find ways of combining them to make 100. Your child will also have experiences with 100 links, 100 seconds, and the *100 Chart*.

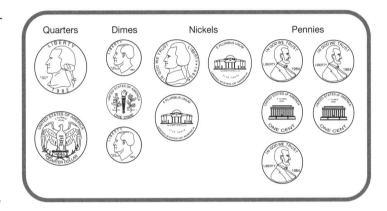

Using coins to make 100

In the lab *Weather 2: Winter Skies*, our class will use the TIMS Laboratory Method to observe daily weather conditions for a winter month.

As we continue to investigate number relationships, you can provide additional support at home by doing some of the following activities:

- *Arrow Dynamics* **Game.** To develop your child's knowledge of number relationships, he or she will play this game in school and bring it home for more practice.
- **Money Counter.** Ask your child to count your loose change each night.
- **Reading Books.** *Picking Peas for a Penny* by Angela Shelf Medaris and *26 Letters and 99 Cents* by Tana Hoban are books featuring coins and their values. Your child may enjoy finding these or other books about coins at the library to read at home.

Thank you for supporting our math activities at home.

Sincerely,

Carta al hogar

Mirando al 100

Fecha: _____

Estimado miembro de familia:

En esta unidad nos concentraremos en el número 100 mientras exploramos las relaciones numéricas en una variedad de contextos.

Su hijo/a usará distintos objetos para "ver" el número 100 y resolver problemas de suma y resta. Por ejemplo, su hijo/a agrupará y contará monedas y buscará maneras de combinarlas para formar 100. Su hijo/a también experimentará con 100 eslabones, 100 segundos, y con la *Tabla 100*.

En la práctica de laboratorio *El tiempo 2: Cielos de invierno,* nuestra clase usará el método de laboratorio TIMS para observar las condiciones climáticas diarias durante un mes del invierno.

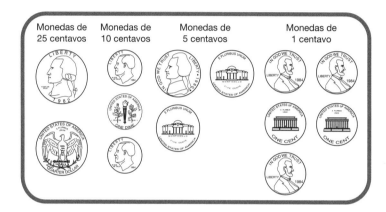

Sumar monedas para formar 100

Mientras seguimos investigando las relaciones numéricas, usted puede dar su apoyo adicional en casa haciendo algunas de las siguientes actividades:

- **Juego de *Dinámica de flechas*.** Para desarrollar el conocimiento de su hijo/a sobre las relaciones numéricas, jugaremos este juego en la escuela y su hijo/a lo llevará a casa para práctica adicional.
- **Contador de dinero.** Pídale a su hijo/a que cuente el cambio que usted tiene todas las noches.
- **Lectura de libros.** *Picking Peas for a Penny* de Angela Shelf Medaris y *26 Letters and 99 Cents* de Tana Hoban son libros que se refieren a las monedas y sus valores. Su hijo/a puede disfrutar buscando éstos u otros libros sobre monedas en la biblioteca para leerlos en casa.

Gracias por el apoyo que brinda en casa a nuestras actividades de matemáticas.

Atentamente,

_____

Table of Contents

Unit 11
Looking at 100

Outline
Looking at 100

Unit Summary

Estimated Class Sessions

II

This unit builds number sense by focusing on the quantity of 100 and extends the partitioning work in Unit 9. A variety of contexts, including time and money, provide problem-solving settings that build ideas about number relationships to 100. This unit includes the second part of the weather lab, *Weather 2: Winter Skies,* which allows students to analyze and compare data collected in Unit 3. An Adventure Book *It's Sunny in Arizona* explores the variability of weather across the United States. The DPP includes items that practice and assess math facts strategies, especially the counting-on strategy.

Major Concept Focus

- money
- exploring the importance of units
- partitioning 100 into two and three parts
- TIMS Laboratory Method
- counting on by fives and tens
- using a calendar
- number relationships
- *Adventure Book:* weather changes
- *100 Chart*
- adding and subtracting with multiples of ten

Pacing Suggestions

Take advantage of *Math Trailblazers®* connections to other subject areas:

- Lesson 6 *Weather 2: Winter Skies* is a laboratory investigation. Students collect weather data in a winter month to compare to the data they collected in the fall in Unit 2 Lesson 6 *Weather 1: Eye on the Sky.* We recommend scheduling this lab in February. Use one math session on the first school day of the month to introduce this lesson. Then, continue to collect data during science time.
- Lesson 7 *It's Sunny in Arizona* is an Adventure Book story that reinforces concepts in the Lesson 6 lab. Read and discuss the story during language arts or social studies.

Assessment Indicators

Use the following Assessment Indicators and the *Observational Assessment Record* that follows the Background section in this unit to assess students on key ideas.

A1. Can students group and count objects by fives and tens?

A2. Can students solve addition and subtraction problems using multiples of five and ten?

A3. Can students partition 100 into groups of tens?

A4. Can students represent numbers using ten frames, *100 Charts,* manipulatives, and number sentences?

A5. Can students find the value of a collection of nickels, dimes, and quarters?

A6. Can students use a calendar to measure the passage of time?

A7. Do students use math facts strategies to add (direct modeling, counting strategies, or reasoning from known facts)?

Unit Planner

	Lesson Information	Supplies	Copies/Transparencies

Lesson 1

100 Links

URG Pages 28–34
SG Page 204
DPP A–B

Estimated Class Sessions
1

Activity
Students partition a 100-link chain into two and three parts. They write addition sentences and describe their partitions.

Assessment
Use Assessment Indicators A1 and A3 and the *Observational Assessment Record* to document students' abilities to count by tens and partition 100 into multiples of ten.

Supplies
- 1 100-link chain per student group
- 1 calculator per student group, optional

Copies/Transparencies
- 1 copy of *Observational Assessment Record* URG Pages 13–14 to be used throughout this unit

Lesson 2

Pennies and Dimes

URG Pages 35–48
SG Pages 205–210
DPP C–F

Estimated Class Sessions
2

Activity
Students explore the relationship between pennies and dimes. They generalize addition and subtraction facts to multiples of ten.

Math Facts Strategies
DPP item E provides addition math facts practice for Group A.

Homework
Assign the *Starting with 100* Homework Pages.

Assessment
Use Assessment Indicators A3 and A4 and the *Observational Assessment Record* to document students' abilities to partition 100 into groups of ten and to represent 100 using ten frames, coins, and number sentences.

Supplies
- 10 pennies per student pair
- 10 dimes per student pair
- overhead pennies and dimes
- scissors, optional

Copies/Transparencies
- 10 pennies or 1 strip from *Pennies Money Master* URG Page 43 per student pair
- 10 dimes or 1 strip from *Dimes Money Master* URG Page 44 per student pair
- 1 transparency of *Ten Frames* URG Page 45
- overhead pennies and dimes or cutouts from transparencies of *Pennies* and *Dimes Money Masters* URG Pages 43–44

Lesson 3

Dimes, Nickels, and Quarters

URG Pages 49–61
SG Pages 211–213
DPP G–J

Estimated Class Sessions
2

Activity
Students compare the values of different coins and determine different combinations of coins that add up to $1.00.

Math Facts Strategies
DPP items G, H, and J provide practice with addition and subtraction math facts.

Homework
Assign the *Shuttle Bus #50* Homework Page as homework or as an assessment.

Assessment
Use Assessment Indicators A2 and A5 and the *Observational Assessment Record* to document students' abilities to use multiples of fives and tens to solve problems and to find the value of a collection of nickels, dimes, and quarters.

Supplies
- scissors
- 10–12 pennies per student pair, optional
- 10 dimes per student pair, optional
- 24–25 nickels per student pair, optional
- 4–5 quarters per student pair, optional
- 1 calculator per student pair, optional
- connecting cubes or other counters, optional
- overhead pennies, nickels, dimes, and quarters

Copies/Transparencies
- 10–12 pennies or 2 strips from *Pennies Money Master* URG Page 43 per student pair, optional
- 10 dimes or 1 strip from *Dimes Money Master* URG Page 44 per student pair, optional
- 24–25 nickels or 3 strips from *Nickels Money Master* URG Page 56 per student pair, optional
- 4–5 quarters or 1 strip from *Quarters Money Master* URG Page 57 per student pair, optional
- extra copies of *100 Chart* URG Page 59 as needed
- 1 transparency of *Arapaho County Fair* URG Page 58
- overhead coins or transparencies of *Pennies, Dimes, Nickels, and Quarters Money Masters* URG Pages 43–44 and 56–57, optional

	Lesson Information	**Supplies**	**Copies/ Transparencies**
Lesson 4 **Arrow Dynamics** URG Pages 62–69 SG Pages 215–223 DPP K–L *Estimated Class Sessions* **1**	**Game** Students develop their knowledge of number relationships by playing the game *Arrow Dynamics* on the *100 Chart* and writing number sentences. **Math Facts Strategies** DPP items K and L provide addition math facts practice. **Homework** 1. The *Who Is Winning?* Activity Page can be used as homework. 2. Have students play *Arrow Dynamics* at home. They will need a *100 Chart* and one copy each of the *Arrow Dynamics Game Board* and *Arrow Dynamics Record Sheet* as well as a spinner (or a paper clip and pencil). **Assessment** 1. Assign the *Follow the Arrows* Assessment Page after playing a few games of *Arrow Dynamics.* 2. Use DPP item L, Assessment Indicator A7, and the *Observational Assessment Record* to document students' abilities to solve the math facts in Group A. Note which strategies students use.	• 1 spinner or paper clip and pencil per student pair • 2 different-colored game markers per student pair	• extra copies of *100 Chart* URG Page 59 as needed • 1 transparency of *Arrow Dynamics Game Board* SG Page 215, optional • 1 transparency of *100 Chart* SG Page 217, optional
Lesson 5 **How Long Is 100?** URG Pages 70–76 SG Page 225 DPP M–N *Estimated Class Sessions* **1**	**Activity** Students discuss seconds and minutes as they develop number sense for 100. They collect and organize data about time. **Math Facts Strategies** DPP item M reviews the value of dimes. DPP item N provides addition math facts practice. **Assessment** Use DPP item N, Assessment Indicator A7, and the *Observational Assessment Record* to document students' use of math facts strategies for the Group A addition facts.	• 1 calculator per student	• 1 transparency of *100 Seconds Class Data Table* URG Page 75
Lesson 6 **Weather 2: Winter Skies** URG Pages 77–93 SG Pages 227–239 DPP O–P *Estimated Class Sessions* **1**	**INTRODUCTORY SESSION** **Lab** Students use the TIMS Laboratory Method to collect, record, and analyze data about weather. They compare data collected in this lesson to data from Unit 2 Lesson 6. **Homework** Use the *Weekend Weather* Blackline Master for homework. Because the time of day must remain constant, students should make their observation times on the blank clock the same as the class time.		• 1 copy of *Weekend Weather* URG Page 88 per student each weekend, optional • 1 transparency of *Weather 2 Graph* SG Page 231 • 1 transparency of *Weather 1 Graph* from Unit 2 Lesson 6 • 1 transparency of *Weather Data* SG Page 235

(Continued)

	Lesson Information	Supplies	Copies/Transparencies
	Assessment 1. Use the *Winter Weather* Assessment Page. 2. Use Assessment Indicator A6 and the *Observational Assessment Record* to document students' abilities to use the calendar to measure the passage of time.		
Lesson 7 **It's Sunny in Arizona** URG Pages 94–102 SG Page 241 AB Pages 41–56 DPP Q–R *Estimated Class Sessions* **1**	**Adventure Book** A family takes a vacation and notes how the weather changes as they travel from state to state.	• crayons	• 1 transparency of *U.S.A Map* SG Page 241, optional
Lesson 8 **Maria's Marble Mart** URG Pages 103–111 SG Pages 242–243 DPP S–V *Estimated Class Sessions* **2**	**Assessment Activity** Students' knowledge of addition and subtraction is assessed as they create and solve problems by grouping and counting with tens. **Math Facts Strategies** DPP item T provides math facts practice. **Assessment** 1. Use the *Marble Orders* Activity Page, Assessment Indicator A2, and the *Observational Assessment Record* to document students' abilities to solve addition problems using multiples of ten. 2. Use the Journal Prompt to assess students' abilities to solve addition problems and describe solution strategies. 3. Transfer appropriate documentation from the *Observational Assessment Record* for Unit 11 to *Individual Assessment Record Sheets*.	• 6 index cards per student pair • 80–100 connecting cubes per student pair • 10 trains of connecting cubes, each containing 10 cubes	• 1 transparency of *Maria's Marble Mart* SG Page 242 • 1 transparency of *Marble Orders* SG Page 243, optional • 1 copy of *Individual Assessment Record Sheet* TIG Assessment section per student, previously copied for use throughout the year

Preparing for Upcoming Lessons

Encourage students to bring quarters to add to the class bank, which will be used throughout the unit's activities.

Connections

A current list of literature and software connections is available at *www.mathtrailblazers.com*. You can also find information on connections in the *Teacher Implementation Guide* Literature List and Software List sections.

Literature Connections

Suggested Titles

- Dee, Ruby. *Two Ways to Count to Ten*. Econo-Clad Books, Topeka, KS, 1999. (Lesson 3)
- Hoban, Tana. *26 Letters and 99 Cents*. Mulberry Books, New York, 1995. (Lesson 3)
- Franco, Betsy. *Many Ways to 100*. Capstone Press, Mankato, MN, 2002.
- Gibbons, Gail. *Weather Forecasting*. Aladdin Books, New York, 1993. (Lesson 6)
- Medearis, Angela Shelf. *Picking Peas for a Penny*. Scholastic Inc., New York, 1993. (Lesson 2)

Software Connections

- *Kid Pix* helps students draw, write, and illustrate math concepts.
- *Math Concepts One . . . Two . . . Three!* provides practice with counting, estimation, comparing and ordering numbers, as well as basic operations (addition and subtraction) with manipulatives and money.
- *Mighty Math Carnival Countdown* provides practice with place value concepts, basic operations (addition and subtraction), and developing the concept of equals and more and less with numbers up to 1000.
- *Mighty Math Zoo Zillions* provides practice with basic operations (addition and subtraction) while manipulating a fish in a tank, rounding, skip counting, and identifying even and odd numbers, as well as word problems.
- *Tenth Network: Grouping and Place Value* practices grouping objects by twos, fives, and tens.
- *Tenth Planet: Combining and Breaking Apart Numbers* provides practice with different number combinations that make up a target number.

Teaching All Math Trailblazers Students

Math Trailblazers lessons are designed for students with a wide range of abilities. The lessons are flexible and do not require significant adaptation for diverse learning styles or academic levels. However, when needed, lessons can be tailored to allow students to engage their abilities to the greatest extent possible while building knowledge and skills.

To assist you in meeting the needs of all students in your classroom, this section contains information about some of the features in the curriculum that allow all students access to mathematics. For additional information, see the Teaching the *Math Trailblazers* Student: Meeting Individual Needs section in the *Teacher Implementation Guide.*

Differentiation Opportunities in this Unit

Games

Use games to promote or extend understanding of math concepts and to practice skills with children who need more practice.

- *Going to Extremes* from Lesson 4 *Arrow Dynamics*

Laboratory Experiments

Laboratory experiments enable students to solve problems using a variety of representations including pictures, tables, graphs, and symbols. Teachers can assign or adapt parts of the analysis according to the student's ability. The following lesson is a lab:

- Lesson 6 *Weather 2: Winter Skies*

Journal Prompts

Journal prompts provide opportunities for students to explain and reflect on mathematical problems. They can help both students who need practice explaining their ideas and students who benefit from answering higher order questions. Students with various learning styles can express themselves using pictures, words, and sentences. Teachers can alter journal prompts to suit students' ability levels. The following lessons contain a journal prompt:

- Lesson 6 *Weather 2: Winter Skies*
- Lesson 8 *Maria's Marble Mart*

Extensions

Use extensions to enrich lessons. Many extensions provide opportunities to further involve or challenge students of all abilities. Take a moment to review the extensions prior to beginning this unit. Some extensions may require additional preparation and planning. The following lessons contain extensions:

- Lesson 1 *100 Links*
- Lesson 3 *Dimes, Nickels, and Quarters*
- Lesson 4 *Arrow Dynamics*
- Lesson 6 *Weather 2: Winter Skies*
- Lesson 7 *It's Sunny in Arizona*
- Lesson 8 *Maria's Marble Mart*

Background
Looking at 100

Number Sense to 100

In this unit, students explore and extend their knowledge of number relationships in a variety of contexts, focusing on the number 100 and multiples of 5 and 10.

The ability to partition numbers is important in developing number sense. It will help children understand part-whole relationships that will be useful when they solve problems and they encounter more formal mathematics.

Several activities in this unit develop this ability by partitioning 10 and 100. Students begin by using 100-link chains to partition 100 into two and three parts. In another activity, they decompose 10 cents using pennies and 100 cents using dimes.

Exploring number relationships in more than one context helps students recognize relationships and generalize patterns. For example, a number sentence such as $10 + 90 = 100$ can be explored using links (10 links + 90 links is 100 links) and using coins (10 cents + 90 cents is 100 cents).

In this unit, students explore the relationship between pennies and dimes. They learn that addition and subtraction facts for 10 can be generalized to multiples of 10, as with the two related number sentences $3 + 7 = 10$ and $30 + 70 = 100$. Research suggests that though children may be able to count by ten, they need additional experiences to make this generalization.

Students use money (nickels and dimes) to partition 100. Children add and subtract multiples of 5 and 10 as they experiment with partitioning $1.00. This activity helps students develop computing methods that will facilitate later number work.

Students use a familiar tool, the *100 Chart,* to expand their number sense. In the game *Arrow Dynamics,* they apply their knowledge of number relationships to write number sentences that describe movements on the *100 Chart.*

Students also extend their knowledge of number relationships by discussing time units (seconds and minutes) as they relate to the number 100. Children experiment with a time duration (100 seconds) and help create and discuss a graph of class data based on each student's performance of a timed task.

Addition Math Facts

In accordance with the *Principles and Standards for School Mathematics, Math Trailblazers* students are expected to achieve fluency with the addition and subtraction facts by the end of second grade. Students in first grade work toward this goal by solving addition and subtraction problems in ways that make sense to them. This use of meaningful strategies enables students to understand the operations, while developing fluency with addition and subtraction facts.

There is a body of research that supports students working toward math facts fluency in this manner. Generally students move through three developmental stages when acquiring operational understanding and fluency with the math facts:

- **Direct Modeling** in which students re-create the action in the problem using manipulatives;
- **Counting Strategies** such as counting on and counting back; and
- **Reasoning from Known Facts** in which students work from facts they know. If, for example, students know that $2 + 2 = 4$, then they have a quick way to access $2 + 3$. (Carpenter, 1999)

The Daily Practice and Problems (DPP) in Units 11 through 20 includes items that provide practice and assess addition facts. The facts are divided into seven groups of eight to ten facts. Each group promotes specific strategies. While the groups of facts may lend themselves to the use of a particular strategy, the emphasis continues to be on students choosing strategies that are meaningful to them and developmentally appropriate. The DPP items in each unit focus on one or more of these groups. Assessment Indicators in Units 11–20 help document students' choice of strategies and their progress toward fluency. See the last Assessment Indicator A7 for this unit and the *Individual*

Assessment Record Sheet in the Assessment section of the *Teacher Implementation Guide.*

For more information, refer to the Daily Practice and Problems Guide for this unit and the TIMS Tutor: *Math Facts* in the *Teacher Implementation Guide.* To inform parents about the curriculum's goals and philosophy of learning and assessing the math facts, send home a copy of *Information for Parents: Grade 1 Math Facts Philosophy* that immediately follows the Background.

"In prekindergarten through grade 2 all students should compute fluently and make reasonable estimates:

- develop strategies for whole-number computations, with a focus on addition and subtraction;

- develop fluency with the basic number combinations for addition and subtraction;

- use a variety of methods and tools to compute, including objects, mental computation, estimation, paper and pencil, and calculators."

From the National Council of Teachers of Mathematics, *Principles and Standards for School Mathematics,* 2000.

Resources

- Baroody, Arthur J. *A Guide to Teaching Mathematics in the Primary Grades.* Allyn and Bacon, Needham Heights, MA, 1989.

- Carpenter, T.P., E. Fennema, M.L. Franke, L. Levi, and S.E. Empson. *Children's Cognitively Guided Instruction.* Heinemann, Westport, CT, 1999.

- Greeno, J.G. "Some Conjectures about Number Sense." In J.T. Sowder & B.P. Schappelle (Eds.), *Establishing Foundations for Research on Number Sense and Related Topics: Report of a Conference,* pp. 43–56. San Diego State University Center for Research in Mathematics and Science Education, San Diego, CA, 1989.

- *Principles and Standards for School Mathematics.* National Council of Teachers of Mathematics, Reston, VA, 2000.

- Thornton, C.A. "Strategies for the Basic Facts." In J.N. Payne (Ed.), *Mathematics for the Young Child.* National Council of Teachers of Mathematics, Reston, VA, 1990.

- Van de Walle, J.A., and Karen Bowman Watkins. "Development of Number Sense." In Robert J. Jensen (Ed.), *Research Ideas for the Classroom: Early Childhood Mathematics,* pp. 127–150. National Council of Teachers of Mathematics, Reston, VA, 1993.

Information for Parents

Grade 1 Math Facts Philosophy

The goal of the math facts strand in *Math Trailblazers* is for students to learn the basic facts efficiently, gain fluency with their use, and retain that fluency over time. In first grade, students focus on addition and subtraction facts strategies. By the end of second grade, students are expected to demonstrate fluency with the addition andF subtraction facts.

A large body of research supports an approach in which students develop strategies for figuring out the facts rather than relying solely on rote memorization. This not only leads to more effective learning and better retention, but also to the development of mental math skills that will be useful throughout life. In fact, too much drill before conceptual understanding may actually interfere with a child's ability to understand concepts at a later date. Therefore, the teaching of the basic facts in *Math Trailblazers* is characterized by the following elements:

Use of Strategies. Students approach the basic facts as problems to be solved rather than as facts to be memorized. In all grades we encourage the use of strategies to find facts and de-emphasize rote memorization, so students become confident that they can find answers to fact problems that they do not immediately recall. In this way, students learn that math is more than memorizing facts and rules which "you either get or you don't."

Distributed Fact Practice. Students study small groups of facts that can be found using similar strategies. Practice of these organized groups of facts begins in the Daily Practice and Problems in Unit 11 and continues for the remainder of the year.

Practice in Context. Students continue to practice all the facts as they use them to solve problems in the labs, activities, and games.

Appropriate Assessment. Units 11–20 include Daily Practice and Problems items that together assess all the addition facts. Students must solve addition fact problems and describe their strategies. Students' progress with the math facts can also be assessed as they complete activities, labs, and games.

Facts Will Not Act as Gatekeepers. Students are not prevented from learning more complex mathematics because they do not have quick recall of the facts. Use of strategies and calculators allows students to continue to work on interesting problems and experiments while they are learning the facts.

Información para los padres

La filosofía de los conceptos matemáticos básicos en 1er grado

El objetivo de la enseñanza de los conceptos matemáticos en *Math Trailblazers* es que los estudiantes aprendan los conceptos básicos eficazmente, logren el dominio del uso de estos conceptos y mantengan ese dominio con el paso del tiempo. En primer grado, los estudiantes se concentran en las estrategias de sumar y restar. Para fines de segundo grado, se espera que los estudiantes demuestren tener dominio de los conceptos básicos de sumar y restar.

Las extensas investigaciones realizadas respaldan la aplicación de un enfoque en el que los estudiantes desarrollan estrategias para resolver los problemas de conceptos básicos en lugar de aprenderlas de memoria. Esto no sólo permite un aprendizaje más eficaz y una mejor retención, sino que también desarrolla habilidades matemáticas mentales que serán útiles durante toda la vida. Por lo tanto, la enseñanza y la evaluación de los conceptos básicos en *Math Trailblazers* se caracteriza por los siguientes elementos:

El uso de estrategias. Los estudiantes enfocan a los conceptos básicos como problemas para resolver en lugar de aprenderlos de memoria. En todos los grados, alentamos el uso de estrategias para hallar soluciones y ponemos menos énfasis en aprender de memoria, de modo que los estudiantes tengan la confianza de que pueden hallar soluciones a problemas de los cuales no se acuerdan. De esta manera, los estudiantes aprenden que las matemáticas son más que tablas y reglas memorizadas que un estudiante "sabe o no sabe".

Repaso gradual de los conceptos básicos. Los estudiantes estudian pequeños grupos de conceptos básicos que pueden hallarse usando estrategias similares. La práctica de estos grupos organizados de conceptos comienza con la Práctica Diaria y los Problemas en la Unidad 11 y continúa el resto del año.

Práctica en contexto. Los estudiantes continúan practicando todos los conceptos básicos cuando los usan para resolver problemas en los experimentos, las actividades y los juegos.

Evaluación apropiada. Las unidades 11–20 incluyen una sección de Práctica Diaria y Problemas que en conjunto permiten evaluar el aprendizaje de todos los conceptos de suma. Los estudiantes deben resolver problemas de suma y describir sus estrategias. El progreso de los estudiantes con los conceptos básicos de suma también puede evaluarse a medida que completan actividades, experimentos y juegos.

El nivel de dominio de los conceptos básicos no impedirá el aprendizaje. Los estudiantes seguirán aprendiendo conceptos matemáticos más complejos aunque no se acuerden de los conceptos básicos con rápidez. El uso de estrategias y calculadoras permite a los estudiantes continuar trabajando con problemas y experimentos interesantes mientras aprenden los conceptos básicos.

Observational Assessment Record

A1 Can students group and count objects by fives and tens?

A2 Can students solve addition and subtraction problems using multiples of five and ten?

A3 Can students partition 100 into groups of tens?

A4 Can students represent numbers using ten frames, *100 Charts,* manipulatives, and number sentences?

A5 Can students find the value of a collection of nickels, dimes, and quarters?

A6 Can students use a calendar to measure the passage of time?

A7 Do students use math facts strategies to add (direct modeling, counting strategies, or reasoning from known facts)?

A8 _____

Name	A1	A2	A3	A4	A5	A6	A7	A8	Comments
1.									
2.									
3.									
4.									
5.									
6.									
7.									
8.									
9.									
10.									
11.									
12.									
13.									

Name	A1	A2	A3	A4	A5	A6	A7	A8	Comments
14.									
15.									
16.									
17.									
18.									
19.									
20.									
21.									
22.									
23.									
24.									
25.									
26.									
27.									
28.									
29.									
30.									
31.									
32.									

Daily Practice and Problems
Looking at 100

A DPP Menu for Unit 11

Two Daily Practice and Problems (DPP) items are included for each class session listed in the Unit Outline. A scope and sequence chart for the DPP is in the *Teacher Implementation Guide*.

Icons in the Teacher Notes column designate the subject matter of each DPP item. Each item falls into one or more of the categories listed below. A menu of the DPP items for Unit 11 follows.

Ⓝ **Number Sense** A–D, F, G, P–R, U, V	▨ **Computation** D, O, U	⧖ **Time**	⬟ **Geometry** I, S
Math Facts **Strategies** E, G, H, J–N, T	$ **Money** C, I, K, M, Q, R	▰ **Measurement** I, S	◩ **Data**

Math Facts Practice

Units 11–20 include DPP items dedicated to working toward fluency with the addition and subtraction facts. The expectation is that students will achieve this fluency by the end of second grade.

The addition facts are organized into groups that promote use of specific strategies. (See the chart below.) However, the DPP items that provide practice with these facts may encourage other ways of thinking about the problems. Encourage students to use strategies that make sense to them.

Unit	Group	Focus Facts
11	A	0 + 1, 1 + 1, 2 + 1, 3 + 1, 0 + 2, 2 + 2, 3 + 2, 4 + 2
12	B	3 + 0, 4 + 0, 5 + 0, 4 + 1, 5 + 1, 6 + 1, 5 + 2, 6 + 2, 5 + 3
13	C	3 + 3, 3 + 4, 4 + 4, 4 + 5, 5 + 5, 5 + 6, 5 + 7, 6 + 6
14	D	1 + 7, 2 + 7, 1 + 8, 2 + 8, 3 + 6, 3 + 7, 3 + 8, 4 + 6, 4 + 7, 4 + 8
15	E	6 + 7, 7 + 7, 7 + 8, 5 + 8, 6 + 8, 8 + 8, 9 + 9, 9 + 10
16	F	9 + 1, 9 + 2, 9 + 3, 9 + 4, 10 + 1, 10 + 2, 10 + 3, 10 + 4
17	G	9 + 5, 9 + 6, 9 + 7, 9 + 8, 10 + 5, 10 + 6, 10 + 7, 10 + 8
18	H	Review Groups A, B, C
19	I	Review Groups D, E
20	J	Review Groups F, G

In this unit, students practice the addition facts for Group A. These facts can be solved by counting on. See DPP items E, H, J, K, L, M, and N for practice with these facts. Items L and N also assess the facts in Group A. Use Assessment Indicator A7

and the *Observational Assessment Record* to document students' progress with these math facts.

For more information about the distribution and assessment of the math facts, see the TIMS Tutor: *Math Facts* in the *Teacher Implementation Guide*.

Daily Practice and Problems

Students may solve the items individually, in groups, or as a class. The items may also be assigned for homework. The DPPs are also available on the Teacher Resource CD.

Student Questions	Teacher Notes

A Skip Counting

1. Skip count by fives to 100 starting at 0.

2. Skip count by fives to 50 starting at 25.

3. Skip count by tens to 100 starting at 0.

4. Skip count by tens to 95 starting at 5.

N

In Lessons 2 and 3, students skip count by fives and tens to find the value of nickels and dimes.

1. 0, 5, 10 . . . 100
2. 25, 30, 35, 40, 45, 50
3. 10, 20, 30 . . . 100
4. 5, 15, 25 . . . 95

B *Spin for Beans 50*

Pam and Heidi played *Spin for Beans 50*. During the game, Pam had 3 full ten frames. Heidi had 4 full ten frames.

1. How many beans did each girl have?

2. How many more beans did Heidi have?

Spin for Beans 50 was introduced in Unit 9 Lesson 3. Students used skip counting by tens (groups of tens and leftovers) to determine the number of beans on their game boards. In Lesson 1 of Unit 11, students skip count by tens to find the number of links in a 100-link chain.

1. Pam had 30 beans. Heidi had 40 beans.

2. 10 beans

C Pennies and Dimes

1. How much are 4 pennies worth?

2. How much are 4 dimes worth?

3. How much are 8 pennies worth?

4. How much are 8 dimes worth?

1. 4¢
2. 40¢
3. 8¢
4. 80¢

D What Is 12?

1. 12 is ten less than _____.

2. 12 is ten more than _____.

3. 12 is six more than _____.

4. 12 is between _____ and _____.

5. 12 is a lot less than _____.

1. 22

2. 2

3. 6

4. Answers will vary.

5. Answers will vary.

E Addition Facts 1

A. 1 + 2 = ☐

B. 2 + 1 = ☐

C. 2 + 3 = ☐

D. 3 + 2 = ☐

E. 1 + 0 = ☐

F. 0 + 1 = ☐

Describe any patterns you see.

A. 3

B. 3

C. 5

D. 5

E. 1

F. 1

Focus discussion on turn-around facts.

Student Questions	Teacher Notes

 F **100 Links**

Nancy broke her 100-link chain into two parts. One chain had 7 groups of ten and the other had 3 groups of ten. Write a number sentence to describe how many links are in both parts of her chain.

Repeat with other partitions.

One possible number sentence:
70 links + 30 links = 100 links

G **How Many in the Bag?**

I have _____ beans in the bag. Now I am taking out _____ beans. How many beans are left in the bag?

What number sentence describes what we just did?

Place an appropriate number of beans (10–20) in the bag. Take out several of the beans to create a subtraction situation. For example, place 18 beans in the bag. Remove 9 beans. Ask students how many are left. An appropriate number sentence for this example is $18 - 9 = 9$. Students were introduced to this activity in Unit 8 Lesson 4 *How Many in the Bag?*

 H **Addition and Subtraction**

1. $2 + 4 = \boxed{}$ 2. $4 + 2 = \boxed{}$

3. $6 - 4 = \boxed{}$ 4. $6 - 2 = \boxed{}$

Discuss your strategies.

1. 6
2. 6
3. 2
4. 4

One possible strategy: using related addition facts to subtract.

I What Is the Area?

1. First use pennies to estimate the area.

2. Then, use quarters to estimate the area.

3. Then, use square-inch tiles to find the area.

1. 8 pennies

2. 6 quarters

3. 6 square inches

Draw a 3-inch by 2-inch rectangle on the overhead. Ask students to predict if all three answers will be the same. Students may predict they will need the greatest number of pennies to cover the rectangle since the penny is the smallest unit of the three. Students did a similar activity for homework on the *Draw a Shape* Homework Page in Unit 10 Lesson 1.

J Addition Facts 2

A. ☐ = 2 + 0

B. 2 + 2 = ☐

C. ☐ = 1 + 1

D. 2 + 4 = ☐

A. 2

B. 4

C. 2

D. 6

It is important for students to understand the meaning of the equals sign. They need to see number sentences where the answer is first.

Student Questions	Teacher Notes

 Pennies and Dimes Again

1. Karen has 3 pennies. Sheila has 1 penny. How much change do they have altogether?

2. Nolan has 3 dimes. Scott has 1 dime. How much change do the boys have altogether?

Each pair of children has 4 coins altogether.

1. Four pennies are worth 4 cents.

2. Four dimes are worth 40 cents. Students may use skip counting to find the answer to Question 2.

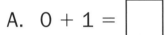 **Addition Facts 3**

A. $0 + 1 = \boxed{}$

B. $1 + 1 = \boxed{}$

C. $1 + 3 = \boxed{}$

D. $2 + 1 = \boxed{}$

Explain how you solved C.

A. 1

B. 2

C. 4

D. 3

Answers will vary. One possible response: counting on by one.

How Many Dimes?

Julie arranged some dimes into two piles. Then, she wrote the following number sentence: 20 cents + 30 cents = 50 cents.

1. How many dimes are in each of Julie's piles?

2. How many dimes does she have in all?

3. How much are all the dimes worth?

In Lesson 2, students partition 10 dimes into two parts and tell the value of each pile.

1. 2 dimes and 3 dimes

2. 5 dimes

3. 50¢

 Addition Facts 4

A. 0 + 2 = ☐

B. 2 + 4 = ☐

C. 2 + 2 = ☐

D. 3 + 2 = ☐

E. 2 + 1 = ☐

Explain how you solved D.

A. 2

B. 6

C. 4

D. 5

E. 3

Answers will vary. One possible response: counting on by two.

Student Questions	Teacher Notes

 Back at the Circus

Twenty-five acrobats were in the ring. Five more joined them. How many acrobats are in the ring now?

Students may use coins to model the addition in this problem.

30 acrobats

 Sharing Peanuts

Jane, her sister, and father shared a bag of peanuts. There were 17 peanuts in the bag. How many peanuts should each person get if they share the peanuts fairly?

Ⓝ

Each person gets 5 peanuts and 2 are left over. Counters should be available for students' use. Some students may prefer to draw a picture to solve the problem.

Nickels and Dimes

1. How many dimes are in 40 cents?

2. How many nickels are in 40 cents?

3. How many dimes are in 70 cents?

4. How many nickels are in 70 cents?

In Lesson 3, students solve problems using nickels and dimes. Since two nickels can be traded for a dime, you need twice the number of nickels as dimes to have the same value. You may demonstrate this trading on the overhead with nickels and dimes.

  1. 4 dimes

  2. 8 nickels

  3. 7 dimes

  4. 14 nickels

R **Nicky and Demi**

1. Nicky has 4 nickels. How much are her coins worth?

2. Demi has 6 dimes. How much are her coins worth?

3. How much money do the two girls have altogether?

Encourage students to share their strategies.

  1. 20¢

  2. 60¢

  3. Since the four nickels can be traded for two dimes, the girls have the same as 8 dimes or 80 cents. Another possible strategy is to start at 60 (60 cents) and skip count by fives (e.g., 65¢, 70¢, 75¢, 80¢).

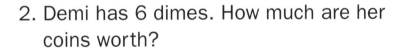

Sally and Tommy

Sally Square is 3 inches by 3 inches.
Tommy Triangle is $4\frac{1}{2}$ square inches.
Which shape has the greater area?

Ask students to suggest ways to solve this problem. Then, use square-inch tiles and half-square-inch pieces to build Sally and Tommy on the overhead. Since Sally covers 9 square inches, she has the greater area.

Sally:

Tommy:

 What's the Weather Like?

1. In Chicago last week, 5 days were sunny and 2 days were cloudy. How many more days were sunny?

2. In Seattle last week, 6 days were cloudy and 1 day was sunny. How many more days were cloudy than sunny?

1. 3 days
2. 5 days

Arrow Dynamics

N ✖

Troy was on 79.
He spun ↓ (+ 10) and then → (+ 1).
Where did he land?

Alex was on 68.
He spun ↓ (+ 10) and then ↓ (+ 10).
Where did he land?

Students were introduced to the game *Arrow Dynamics* in Lesson 4. Have a transparency of a *100 Chart* available to show the moves.

1. Troy: 79 + 10 + 1 = 90
   Alex: 68 + 10 + 10 = 88

2. Troy

1. Write a number sentence for Troy's moves and another for Alex's moves.

2. Who is winning?

 Numbers

N

1. What number is two more than 11?

2. What number is three less than 7?

3. What number is one more than 19?

4. Name an even number between 4 and 10.

5. Name an even number between 10 and 15.

In Unit 9 Lesson 5, students explored patterns when skip counting by twos. One pattern they may have discovered is that even numbers are numbers we reach when skip counting by twos. Other work with even numbers took place in Unit 4 Lesson 1.

1. 13
2. 4
3. 20
4. 6 or 8
5. 12 or 14

Lesson 1

100 Links

Estimated Class Sessions

1

Lesson Overview

Students work in groups with chain links grouped by tens in alternating colors. They practice counting by tens. Students partition 100 into two and three parts using the links and write number sentences that describe their partitions.

Key Content

- Representing 100 with links.
- Grouping and counting objects by tens.
- Partitioning 100 into multiples of ten.
- Exploring the relationship between addition facts for ten and multiples of ten.
- Writing number sentences for addition situations.

Assessment

Use Assessment Indicators A1 and A3 and the *Observational Assessment Record* to document students' abilities to count by tens and partition 100 into multiples of ten.

Curriculum Sequence

Before This Unit

In Unit 9 Lesson 5 *100 Chart* students skip counted by tens and discovered patterns using the *100 Chart*.

Materials List

Supplies and Copies

Student	Teacher
Supplies for Each Student Group • 100-link chain (See Before the Activity) • calculator, optional	**Supplies**
Copies	**Copies/Transparencies** • 1 copy of *Observational Assessment Record* to be used throughout this unit (*Unit Resource Guide* Pages 13–14)

All blackline masters including assessment, transparency, and DPP masters are also on the Teacher Resource CD.

Student Books
100-Link Chain (*Student Guide* Page 204)

Daily Practice and Problems
DPP items A–B (*Unit Resource Guide* Pages 17–18)

Assessment Tools
Observational Assessment Record (*Unit Resource Guide* Pages 13–14)

Daily Practice and Problems

Suggestions for using the DPPs are on page 32.

A. Skip Counting (URG p. 17) [N]

1. Skip count by fives to 100 starting at 0.

2. Skip count by fives to 50 starting at 25.

3. Skip count by tens to 100 starting at 0.

4. Skip count by tens to 95 starting at 5.

B. *Spin for Beans 50* (URG p. 18) [N]

Pam and Heidi played *Spin for Beans 50*. During the game, Pam had 3 full ten frames. Heidi had 4 full ten frames.

1. How many beans did each girl have?

2. How many more beans did Heidi have?

Sort the links into groups of 50 of the same color. Each group of students will need two different-colored sets of 50 links so they can make chains with groups of 10 in alternating colors.

Teaching the Activity

Part 1 Partitioning 100 into Two Parts

Assign students to groups of four. Distribute two different-colored sets of 50 links to each group. Have groups sort the links into groups of 10 and then make a chain of 100 links by alternating colors every 10 links. Have group members check the lengths of their chains by comparing them to other groups' chains. Ask:

- *How many groups of ten links make up your chain?* (10 groups)
- *Count the number of links in your chain by skip counting by tens.* (100 links)

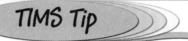

Relate the 10 rows on the *100 Chart* to the 10 groups of ten in their 100-link chains.

Ask each group to break their chain into two parts, but only where one color stops and the new color starts (they cannot break the chain within a group of ten). Tell students that the two parts do not have to be equal. Ask groups to count the number of links in each part and write a corresponding number sentence on the *100-Link Chain* Activity Page. Encourage students to skip count by tens to determine the number of links in each part. Students can use calculators to check that the two partitions in their number sentences add up to 100.

Ask one group to display the two parts of their 100-link chain to the class. Ask questions such as the following to relate addition sentences with multiples of ten (20 + 80 = 100) to basic addition facts for ten (2 + 8 = 10).

- *Show us one of the two parts. How many groups of ten are in your first part?* (2 groups of ten)
- *Show us the other part. How many groups of ten are in your second part?* (8 groups of ten)
- *How many groups of ten were there in the one long chain?* (10 groups of ten)

TIMS Tip

A 100-link chain is quite long. If possible, use an open area for this activity.

Name _____ Date _____

100-Link Chain

Two Parts
Break your chain into two parts. Count the number of links in each part. Then, write a number sentence.

_____ + _____ = _____

Three Parts
Break your chain into three parts. Count the number of links in each part. Then, write a number sentence.

_____ + _____ + _____ = _____

Find three more ways to break the chain into three parts. Write a number sentence for each.

_____ + _____ + _____ = _____

_____ + _____ + _____ = _____

_____ + _____ + _____ = _____

204 SG • Grade 1 • Unit 11 • Lesson 1   100 Links

Student Guide - page 204 *(Answers on p. 34)*

- *Do you still have all the links? How can you be sure?* (2 groups of ten + 8 groups of ten = 10 groups of ten)

- *How many links are in the first part?* (20 links; ask a student from another group to check.)

- *How many links are in the second part?* (80 links; ask another student to skip count by tens to check.)

- *What number sentence did you write?* (20 + 80 = 100; record this number sentence on the board.)

Ask other groups to share their number sentences and chains with the class. Record the different number sentences on the board. If you notice that a particular number sentence is missing, hold up the partition, such as 3 groups of ten, and ask:

- *What if one part had 3 groups of ten? How many links would be in that part?* (30 links)

- *How many groups of ten would be in the other part?* (7 groups; 3 groups of ten + 7 groups of ten = 10 groups of ten) Encourage students to use their chains to answer this question.

- *How many links would be in this second part?* (70 links)

- *What number sentence would describe this partition?* (30 + 70 = 100)

While students share their solutions, a discussion may arise as to whether two number sentences such as 20 + 80 = 100 and 80 + 20 = 100 are the same or different solutions. Ask individuals for their opinions. Have these students explain why they consider the sentences different or the same. Then, come to a class agreement.

To conclude, ask students questions such as:

- *What is the same about these number sentences?* (They add up to 100. They have two parts.)

- *What is the same about all our partitions?* (They have groups of ten in them. The two parts add up to 100.)

- *If I have 1 group of ten and 9 groups of ten, how many links do I have in each part?* (10 links and 90 links)

- *What number sentences describe this partition?* (1 group of ten + 9 groups of ten = 10 groups; 10 links + 90 links = 100 links)

Part 2 Partitioning 100 into Three Parts

Ask student groups to reassemble their 100-link chains before starting this part. Then, ask them to partition their 100-link chains into *three* parts and record a number sentence that describes the partition on the *100-Link Chain* Activity Page. Tell students to find as many different partitions as possible, breaking the chains only between colors. They should reassemble their 100-link chain before they try to find each different partition. Remind them to record each number sentence on the *100-Link Chain* Activity Page. Space is provided for four sentences. If a group finds more than four different partitions before time runs out, recommend that they record the others in the blank space on the activity page or on a separate sheet of paper.

Homework and Practice

DPP item A provides skip counting practice by fives and tens. Item B reviews the game *Spin for Beans 50.*

Assessment

Observe students as they partition their chain links and skip count to find the number of links in each partition. Use the *Observational Assessment Record* to document students' abilities to count by tens and partition 100 into multiples of ten.

Extension

Students may partition their 100-link chains into four or more parts and record number sentences that describe their partitions.

At a Glance

Math Facts Strategies and Daily Practice and Problems

DPP items A and B develop number sense using multiples of five and ten.

Part 1. Partitioning 100 into Two Parts

1. Distribute two different-colored sets of 50 links to each group of four students.
2. Students sort the links into groups of 10 and then make a chain of 100 links by alternating colors in groups of 10.
3. Group members check the lengths of their chains by comparing them to other groups' chains.
4. Students skip count by tens to find the total number of links in each chain.
5. Students break their chain into two parts at the end of one color, count the number of links in each part, and write a corresponding number sentence on the *100-Link Chain* Activity Page.
6. A group of students displays the two parts of their 100-link chain to the class. Discuss their partitions and number sentence. Relate their addition sentence with multiples of ten (20 + 80 = 100) to basic addition facts for ten (2 + 8 = 10).
7. Other groups share their number sentences and chains with the class. Record the different number sentences on the board.

Part 2. Partitioning 100 into Three Parts (A1) (A2) (A3)

1. Student groups reassemble their 100-link chains.
2. Students partition their 100-link chains into three parts and record a number sentence that describes the partition on the *100-Link Chain* Activity Page.
3. Students try to find as many different partitions as possible.

Assessment

Use *Assessment Indicators* A1 and A3 and the *Observational Assessment Record* to document students' abilities to count by tens and partition 100 into multiples of ten.

Extension

Have students partition their 100-link chains into parts and record number sentences.

Answer Key is on page 34.

Notes:

Name _____ Date _____

100-Link Chain

Two Parts

Break your chain into two parts. Count the number of links in each part. Then, write a number sentence.

_____ + _____ = _____

Three Parts

Break your chain into three parts. Count the number of links in each part. Then, write a number sentence.

_____ + _____ + _____ = _____

Find three more ways to break the chain into three parts. Write a number sentence for each.

_____ + _____ + _____ = _____

_____ + _____ + _____ = _____

_____ + _____ + _____ = _____

Copyright © Kendall/Hunt Publishing Company

204 SG • Grade 1 • Unit 11 • Lesson 1   100 Links

Student Guide - page 204

Student Guide (p. 204)

100-Link Chain

Answers will vary.*

*Answers and/or discussion are included in the Lesson Guide.

Lesson 2

Pennies and Dimes

Lesson Overview

Estimated Class Sessions
2

Students divide groups of 10 pennies into equal and unequal piles. They do the same using dimes and multiples of ten. Then they write addition and subtraction sentences to represent the number combinations of their coin piles.

Key Content

- Translating between different representations of numbers (ten frames, coins, number sentences).
- Exploring the relationship between addition and subtraction facts and adding multiples of ten.
- Partitioning ten and 100 into two and three parts.
- Finding the value of a collection of dimes.

Math Facts Strategies

DPP item E provides addition math facts practice for Group A.

Homework

Assign the *Starting with 100* Homework Pages.

Assessment

Use Assessment Indicators A3 and A4 and the *Observational Assessment Record* to document students' abilities to partition 100 into groups of ten and to represent 100 using ten frames, coins, and number sentences.

Curriculum Sequence

Before This Unit

Ten Frames

Students represented numbers using ten frames in Units 3, 5, 8, and 9.

Coins

Students used pennies in ten frames to represent numbers in Unit 3. They worked with pennies, nickels, and dimes in Unit 5 Lesson 2.

Materials List

Supplies and Copies

Student	Teacher
Supplies for Each Student Pair • 10 pennies or 1 strip from *Pennies Money Master* (*Unit Resource Guide* Page 43) • 10 dimes or 1 strip from *Dimes Money Master* (*Unit Resource Guide* Page 44)	**Supplies** • overhead pennies and dimes or cutouts from transparencies of *Pennies Money Master* and *Dimes Money Master* (*Unit Resource Guide* Pages 43–44) • scissors, optional
Copies	**Copies/Transparencies** • 1 transparency of *Ten Frames* (*Unit Resource Guide* Page 45)

All blackline masters including assessment, transparency, and DPP masters are also on the Teacher Resource CD.

Student Books

Pennies (*Student Guide* Page 205)
Dimes (*Student Guide* Page 206)
Three Piles (*Student Guide* Page 207)
Starting with 100 (*Student Guide* Pages 209–210)

Daily Practice and Problems

DPP items C–F (*Unit Resource Guide* Pages 18–20)

Assessment Tools

Observational Assessment Record (*Unit Resource Guide* Pages 13–14)

Daily Practice and Problems

Suggestions for using the DPPs are on pages 40–41.

C. Pennies and Dimes (URG p. 18)

1. How much are 4 pennies worth?
2. How much are 4 dimes worth?
3. How much are 8 pennies worth?
4. How much are 8 dimes worth?

D. What Is 12? (URG p. 19)

1. 12 is ten less than _____.
2. 12 is ten more than _____.
3. 12 is six more than _____.
4. 12 is between _____ and _____.
5. 12 is a lot less than _____.

E. Addition Facts 1 (URG p. 19)

A. $1 + 2 =$ ☐

B. $2 + 1 =$ ☐

C. $2 + 3 =$ ☐

D. $3 + 2 =$ ☐

E. $1 + 0 =$ ☐

F. $0 + 1 =$ ☐

Describe any patterns you see.

F. 100 Links (URG p. 20)

Nancy broke her 100-link chain into two parts. One chain had 7 groups of ten and the other had 3 groups of ten. Write a number sentence to describe how many links are in both parts of her chain.

Encourage students to bring in pennies for the class bank. Each pair of students will need 10 pennies. If real coins are not available, copy and cut out the coin strips of pennies and dimes provided on the *Pennies Money Master* and *Dimes Money Master* Blackline Masters.

Part 1 Partitioning 10 Pennies

Remind students of their work with ten frames in Unit 3 Lesson 2. In that lesson several beans were placed on a ten frame. Students wrote number sentences that described the number of beans. Place ten overhead pennies on a ten frame on the *Ten Frames* transparency. Ask students:

- *How many cents is this?* (10¢)

Remove three pennies and ask students to write an addition or a subtraction number sentence that describes the ten frame. To focus students' attention on partitions of 10, ask them for addition or subtraction sentences that include 10.

Students may write, for example, $10 - 3 = 7$ or $7 + 3 = 10$. Repeat several times using a different number of pennies each time.

Figure 1: *Possible number sentences for this ten frame are $10 - 3 = 7$ or $7 + 3 = 10$*

In Unit 3 Lesson 6 students partitioned 10 into two and three parts using pennies and pockets. Students will again partition 10 in this activity to prepare them for similar work with dimes in Part 2. Working with pennies first and then dimes will help students generalize addition and subtraction facts for ten (e.g., $3 + 7 = 10$) to multiples of ten $(30 + 70 = 100)$.

Give each student pair 10 pennies or cutouts of pennies from the *Pennies Money Master* Blackline Master. Then, ask the pairs to divide their group of pennies into two piles. Ask:

- *How many pennies are in each pile?*
- *What is each pile worth in cents?*

Name _____ Date _____

Pennies

You have 10 pennies to put into two piles. Do this in many ways. Write a number sentence for each. Then, put the 10 pennies into 3 piles. Write a number sentence.

Pennies
_____ + _____ = 10
_____ + _____ = 10
_____ + _____ = 10
10 = _____ + _____
10 = _____ + _____
10 − _____ = _____
10 − _____ = _____
10 − _____ = _____
_____ + _____ + _____ = 10

Pennies and Dimes   SG • Grade 1 • Unit 11 • Lesson 2   205

Student Guide - page 205 *(Answers on p. 46)*

Ask students to record a number sentence for their partition on the *Pennies* Activity Page. The number sentence should show the number of pennies (cents) in each pile (e.g., 5 + 5 = 10). Encourage them to find more ways to divide the pennies into two piles and record addition and subtraction number sentences for each on the *Pennies* Activity Page (e.g., 1 + 9 = 10; 2 + 8 = 10; 10 − 3 = 7; 10 − 4 = 6). Finally, ask students to partition the pennies into three piles and record a number sentence on the *Pennies* Activity Page. Record students' answers on the board as they share them with the class.

Part 2 Partitioning 10 Dimes

Place ten dimes on a ten frame on the *Ten Frames* transparency. Ask:

- *How much is ten dimes worth?* Students can skip count by tens to determine that 10 dimes is the same as 100 cents.

You can relate the 10 dimes in 100 cents to the ten rows in the *100 Chart*. Also, in the previous activity students linked 10 groups of ten links to form a 100-link chain.

Place eight dimes on a ten frame on the *Ten Frames* transparency. Emphasize the relationship between the addition sentence 8 + 2 = 10 and 80 + 20 = 100. Ask:

- *How many dimes are there?* (8)
- *What is a number sentence that describes how many more dimes are needed to have 10 dimes?* (8 + 2 = 10 dimes)
- *What is the value of the dimes on the ten frame? How many cents are 8 dimes worth?* (80 cents)
- *What is a number sentence that describes the amount of change on the ten frame if we were to add two more dimes?* (80 + 20 = 100 cents)

Next, place 10 dimes on a ten frame. Then, take 3 away. Ask questions similar to the following:

- *How many dimes did I start with?* (10 dimes)
- *How many did I take away?* (3 dimes)
- *How many do I have left?* (7 dimes)
- *How much change did I start with? What were the 10 dimes worth?* (100 cents)
- *How much change did I take away? What were the 3 dimes worth?* (30 cents)
- *How much change do I have left? What are the 7 dimes worth?* (70 cents; students may skip count by tens to find the answer.)
- *What number sentence describes the amount of change left on this ten frame?* (100 − 30 = 70 cents)

Content Note

Units. As students say number sentences that describe the dimes on the ten frame, encourage them to use the proper unit. If I place 6 dimes on a ten frame and say 60 + 40 = 100, I am referring to the *value* of the coins. That is, 60 cents + 40 cents = 100 cents. If I say 6 + 4 = 10, I am referring to the *number* of coins. That is 6 dimes + 4 dimes = 10 dimes.

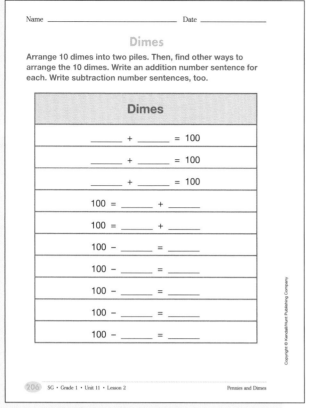

Student Guide - page 206 *(Answers on p. 46)*

Student Guide - page 207 *(Answers on p. 47)*

Distribute 10 dimes or cutouts of dimes from the *Dimes Money Master* Blackline Master to each student pair. Then, ask the pairs to divide their dimes into two piles. Ask a pair to help you count their piles by tens to find the value of the dimes in each (e.g., 10, 20, 30, 40, 50). Then, have them write an addition number sentence to show the value of each pile, as they did with pennies. They should record this sentence on the *Dimes* Activity Page. Other student pairs should do the same. Remind students that they are recording the value of the dimes, not the number of dimes (e.g., 50 + 50 = 100 not 5 + 5 = 10).

Next, ask students to find other ways to divide the group of dimes into two piles. Also, invite them to write subtraction sentences as well. In the above example, a student could start with two piles of 50 and cover up one pile. An appropriate number sentence for this partition is 100 − 50 = 50. Have them write their number sentences on the chart on the *Dimes* Activity Page. Record students' answers on the board as they share them with the class.

Students will have more opportunities to practice this activity on the *Starting with 100* Homework Pages.

Part 3 Partitioning 10 Dimes into Three Parts
Ask students to divide their group of dimes into three piles. As before, encourage them to find as many different combinations as they can. They should record number sentences for the combinations on the *Three Piles* Activity Page. Discuss the results as before.

Math Facts Strategies

- DPP item E practices the addition math facts for Group A and explores turn-around facts. Students can use a counting-on strategy to solve the facts in Group A.
- Using ten frames to partition ten pennies into two parts in Part 1 of this lesson provides practice with the facts that make a ten.

- To give students more practice writing addition and subtraction sentences with dimes, assign the *Starting with 100* Homework Pages. To fill in the missing addends, students may place counters or real dimes on the strip of dimes and skip count to find the value of the uncovered or remaining dimes. A strip of dimes is also provided at the bottom of the first page. Students may cut out these dimes and use them to find the solutions. Discuss their answers as a group the following class period.

- DPP item C practices finding the value of pennies and dimes. Item D develops number sense using the number 12. Item F uses links to partition 100 into multiples of ten.

Assessment

Use the *Observational Assessment Record* to document students' abilities to partition 100 into two and three parts and to represent 100 using ten frames, coins, and number sentences.

Literature Connection

Medearis, Angela S. *Picking Peas for a Penny.* Scholastic Inc., New York, 1993.

This book is a rhyming text about an African-American farm family picking peas during the Great Depression. The children are promised one penny for each pound of peas they pick.

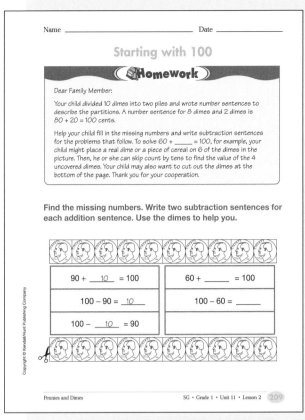

Student Guide - page 209 *(Answers on p. 47)*

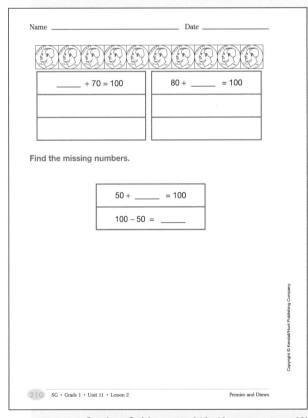

Student Guide - page 210 *(Answers on p. 48)*

At a Glance

Math Facts Strategies and Daily Practice and Problems

DPP item E practices addition math facts for Group A. Items C, D, and F build number sense.

Part 1. Partitioning 10 Pennies

1. Place ten pennies on the *Ten Frames* transparency. Ask students, *"How many cents is this?"* (10¢)
2. Remove three pennies. Students write addition or subtraction sentences that describe the ten frame.
3. Repeat this procedure several times using a different number of pennies each time.
4. Assign students to pairs, and give each pair ten pennies or ten pennies from the *Pennies Money Master* Blackline Master.
5. Student pairs divide their ten pennies into piles and record a number sentence on the *Pennies* Activity Page.
6. Students find more ways to divide the pennies into two and three piles and record addition and subtraction sentences for each on the *Pennies* Activity Page.
7. Record students' answers on the chalkboard as they share them with the class.

Part 2. Partitioning 10 Dimes (A2) (A3) (A4)

1. Place ten dimes on the *Ten Frames* transparency. Students skip count by tens to determine that ten dimes is the same as 100 cents.
2. Place eight dimes on a ten frame. Students discuss the number and value of the coins and determine an addition number sentence.
3. Place ten dimes on a ten frame. Then, take 3 away. Students determine a subtraction number sentence describing the ten frame and the value of the remaining coins.
4. Distribute ten dimes or ten dimes from the *Dimes Money Master* Blackline Master to each student pair.
5. Students divide their ten dimes into two piles.
6. Students write an addition number sentence on the *Dimes* Activity Page to show the value of each pile.
7. Students find other ways to divide the group of dimes into two piles. They write addition and subtraction sentences that represent their partitions.

Part 3. Partitioning 10 Dimes into Three Parts

Students divide their ten dimes into three piles and record number sentences on the *Three Piles* Activity Page. Discuss the results.

Homework

Assign the *Starting with 100* Homework Pages.

Assessment

Use Assessment Indicators A3 and A4 and the *Observational Assessment Record* to document students' abilities to partition 100 into groups of ten and to represent 100 using ten frames, coins, and number sentences.

Connection

Read and discuss *Picking Peas for a Penny* by Angela S. Medearis.

Answer Key is on pages 46–48.

Notes:

Pennies Money Master

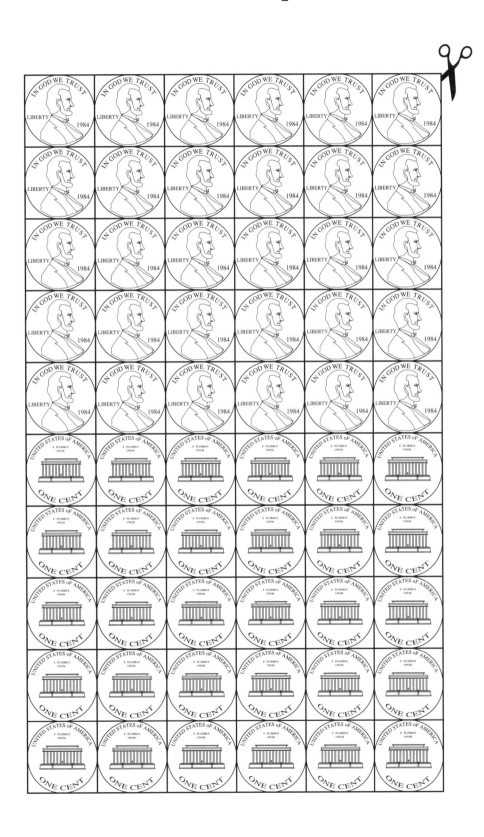

Dimes Money Master

Ten Frames

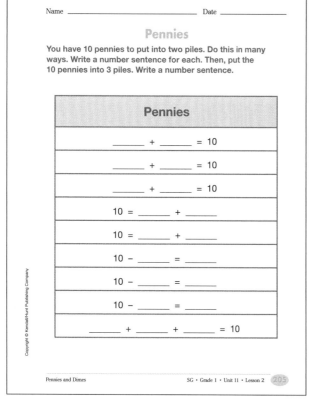

Student Guide - page 205

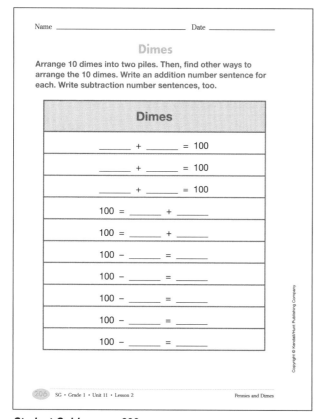

Student Guide - page 206

Student Guide (p. 205)

Pennies

Answers will vary. Some possible addition number sentences are: $0 + 10 = 10$, $1 + 9 = 10$, $2 + 8 = 10$, $10 = 3 + 7$, $10 = 4 + 6$, and $5 + 5 = 10$. Some possible subtraction number sentences are: $10 - 0 = 10$, $10 - 9 = 1$, $10 - 8 = 2$, $10 - 7 = 3$, $10 - 6 = 4$, and $10 - 5 = 5$. One possible 3 pile addition number sentence is $1 + 2 + 7 = 10$.

Student Guide (p. 206)

Dimes

Answers will vary. Some possible addition number sentences are: $0 + 100 = 100$, $10 + 90 = 100$, $20 + 80 = 100$, $100 = 30 + 70$, $100 = 40 + 60$, and $50 + 50 = 100$. Some possible subtraction number sentences are: $100 - 0 = 100$, $100 - 90 = 10$, $100 - 80 = 20$, $100 - 70 = 30$, $100 - 60 = 40$, and $100 - 50 = 50$.

Student Guide (p. 207)

Three Piles

Answers will vary. Some possible number sentences include: $10 + 10 + 80 = 100$, $10 + 20 + 70 = 100$, $10 + 30 + 60 = 100$, $10 + 40 + 50 = 100$, $20 + 20 + 60 = 100$, $20 + 30 + 50 = 100$, $20 + 40 + 40 = 100$, and $30 + 30 + 40 = 100$.

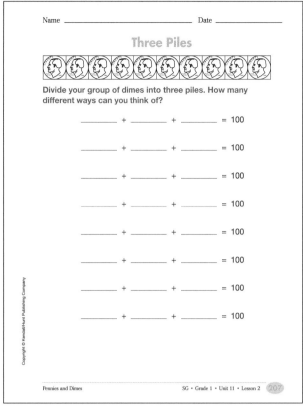

Student Guide - page 207

Student Guide (p. 209)

Starting with 100*

$60 + 40 = 100$

$100 - 60 = 40$

$100 - 40 = 60$

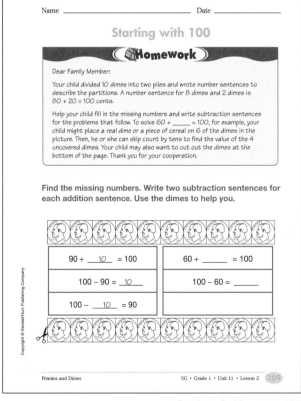

Student Guide - page 209

*Answers and/or discussion are included in the Lesson Guide.

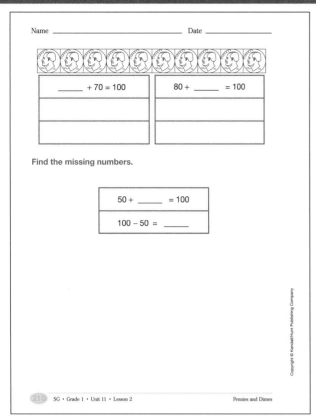

Student Guide - page 210

Student Guide (p. 210)*

$30 + 70 = 100$ $80 + 20 = 100$

$100 - 30 = 70$ $100 - 80 = 20$

$100 - 70 = 30$ $100 - 20 = 80$

$50 + 50 = 100$

$100 - 50 = 50$

*Answers and/or discussion are included in the Lesson Guide.

Lesson 3

Dimes, Nickels, and Quarters

Lesson Overview

Estimated Class Sessions

2

Students review and compare values of pennies, nickels, dimes, and quarters. They compare how long it takes to count using pennies to how long it takes to count using larger coins. Students discuss the usefulness of using coins with higher values. Finally, they determine different combinations of coins that add up to 100.

Key Content

- Grouping and counting a collection of coins by fives and tens.
- Solving problems using multiples of fives and tens.
- Partitioning 100 ($1.00) into two and three parts using coins.
- Translating between representations of numbers (coins and number sentences).
- Introducing the value of a quarter.
- Finding the value of a collection of nickels, dimes, and quarters.

Math Facts Strategies

DPP items G, H, and J provide practice with addition and subtraction math facts.

Homework

Assign the *Shuttle Bus #50* Homework Page as homework or as an assessment.

Assessment

Use Assessment Indicators A2 and A5 and the *Observational Assessment Record* to document students' abilities to use multiples of fives and tens to solve problems and to find the value of a collection of nickels, dimes, and quarters.

Materials List

Supplies and Copies

Student	Teacher
Supplies for Each Student Pair	**Supplies**
• 10–12 pennies or 2 strips from *Pennies Money Master,* optional (*Unit Resource Guide* Page 43) • 10 dimes or 1 strip from *Dimes Money Master,* optional (*Unit Resource Guide* Page 44) • 24–25 nickels or 3 strips from *Nickels Money Master,* optional (*Unit Resource Guide* Page 56) • 4–5 quarters or 1 strip from *Quarters Money Master,* optional (*Unit Resource Guide* Page 57) • calculators, optional • connecting cubes or other counters, optional	• overhead pennies, nickels, dimes, and quarters or cutouts from transparencies of *Pennies, Nickels, Dimes,* and *Quarters Money Masters* (*Unit Resource Guide* Pages 43–44 and 56–57) • scissors
Copies	**Copies/Transparencies**
• extra copies of *100 Chart* as needed (*Unit Resource Guide* Page 59)	• 1 transparency of *Arapaho County Fair* (*Unit Resource Guide* Page 58)

All blackline masters including assessment, transparency, and DPP masters are also on the Teacher Resource CD.

Student Books
Twins' Day at the County Fair (*Student Guide* Page 211)
Shuttle Bus #100 (*Student Guide* Page 212)
Shuttle Bus #50 (*Student Guide* Page 213)

Daily Practice and Problems
DPP items G–J (*Unit Resource Guide* Pages 20–21)

Assessment Tools
Observational Assessment Record (*Unit Resource Guide* Pages 13–14)

G. How Many in the Bag? (URG p. 20)

I have ___ beans in the bag. Now I am taking out ___ beans. How many beans are left in the bag?

What number sentence describes what we just did?

H. Addition and Subtraction (URG p. 20)

1. 2 + 4 = ☐
2. 4 + 2 = ☐
3. 6 − 4 = ☐
4. 6 − 2 = ☐

Discuss your strategies.

I. What Is the Area? (URG p. 21)

1. First use pennies to estimate the area.
2. Then, use quarters to estimate the area.
3. Then, use square-inch tiles to find the area.

J. Addition Facts 2 (URG p. 21)

A. ☐ = 2 + 0
B. 2 + 2 = ☐
C. ☐ = 1 + 1
D. 2 + 4 = ☐

Part 1 Coins

Begin by giving a volunteer 100 pennies and asking the student to give you 30¢. When the student is finished, point out to the class how long it takes to count individual pennies. Ask them to imagine how long it would take to count out 100 pennies. Now, have another child hold 10 dimes, reminding students that a dime is worth 10 cents, or 10 pennies. Ask the student to give you 30¢ in dimes. Point out how much faster it is to count by tens to 30 than by ones to 30. Discuss:

- *Why is it useful to have coins of higher value than pennies?*

- *Name coins other than pennies or dimes that are commonly used. How much are they worth in cents?* (nickel—5¢, quarter—25¢)

Make sure students understand the value of each coin in terms of pennies (e.g., a quarter is the same as 25 pennies). Pose and discuss the following questions:

- *If we had nickels instead of dimes, how many nickels would we need for 30¢?* (6)

- *How many dimes are the same value as 100 pennies?* (10)

- *How many nickels are the same value as 100 pennies?* (20)

- *How many quarters are the same value as 100 pennies?* (4)

You can use the overhead coins to show students different combinations of coins for amounts that you specify. For example, ask:

- *Show me some possible coin combinations for 20 cents on the overhead projector.* (20 pennies; 4 nickels; 2 dimes; 10 pennies and 2 nickels; 10 pennies and 1 dime; 5 pennies, 1 dime, and 1 nickel; 15 pennies and 1 nickel; 5 pennies and 3 nickels).

Make sure students can create the different combinations for a quarter. Encourage students to use coins to help them think of different combinations. Students can use calculators to check their answers or to try out different combinations.

Read the following paragraphs to students as an introduction to the *Twins' Day at the County Fair* Activity Page.

> *It's Twins' Day at the Arapaho County Fair. Sets of twins can participate in any event for the price of one ticket. Every event costs $1.00.*

Arapaho County Fair

Ferris Wheel....... $1.00

Balloon Toss...... $1.00

Target Range..... $1.00

Bumper Cars...... $1.00

Petting Zoo.........$1.00

Figure 2: *$1.00 events at the Arapaho County Fair*

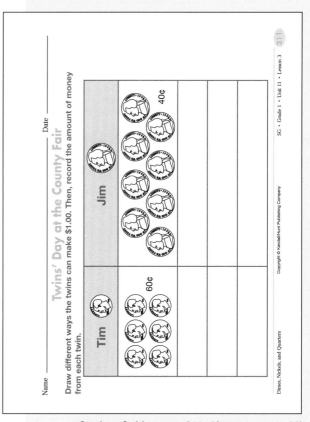

Student Guide - page 211 *(Answers on p. 60)*

> *Gramps thinks it's a good day to take the twins, Tim and Jim, to the County Fair. He gives a stack of coins to each. Tim has dimes and Jim has nickels. Gramps tells them there are some rules they have to follow to share the cost of each ticket:*
>
> 1. *Each twin must contribute at least one coin for each ticket.*
> 2. *They must use a different combination of coins for each ticket.*
> 3. *They must keep a record of how they spend their money.*
> 4. *The coins the twins give must add up to $1.00.*
>
> *The twins thank Gramps and agree to meet him at the Lemonade Stand at 12:30 for lunch. They are eager to buy tickets, but need some help. Let's help Tim and Jim.*

Display a transparency of the *Arapaho County Fair* Transparency Master, which reiterates Gramps's rules. Have student pairs record on the *Twins' Day at the County Fair* Activity Page different ways the twins can combine the coins to make $1.00. Circulate around the room to make sure all students understand the assignment. When everyone is finished, invite students to share their answers with the class. Write some of the combinations on the board and discuss them as a group.

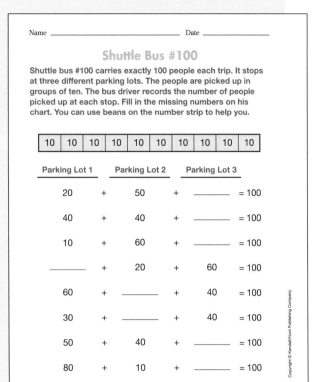

Student Guide - page 212 *(Answers on p. 60)*

Student Guide - page 213 *(Answers on p. 61)*

Students may practice working with multiples of ten with the *Shuttle Bus #100* Activity Page. Encourage them to tell the strategies they use to find the number of people in each parking lot. Students can use counters and place them over the number strip on the activity page to find missing addends, they can use a calculator, a *100 Chart,* or they might skip count by tens to 100.

Math Facts Strategies

DPP item G provides practice with subtraction facts by reviewing the activity *How Many in the Bag?* Items H and J provide practice with the addition math facts in Group A. Item H relates addition and subtraction strategies.

Homework and Practice

*   Give students more practice working with multiples of five by assigning the *Shuttle Bus #50* Homework Page. This page can also be used as an assessment.

*   DPP item I provides practice with measuring area. First, students estimate the area of a rectangle using pennies and quarters. Then, they find the area using square-inch tiles.

Assessment

Use the *Observational Assessment Record* to document students' abilities to solve addition problems using multiples of five and ten to find the value of a collection of nickels, dimes, and quarters.

Extension

Have students skip count by ones on a calculator as fast as they can for 10 seconds. If students have a calculator with a hot equals key (a constant function), they can push 1 + 1 = = =. Students then estimate what number will be in the window if they skip counted by fives for ten seconds. Try it. Then, repeat with tens and twenty-fives.

Literature Connections

*   Dee, Ruby. *Two Ways to Count to Ten.* Econo-Clad Books, Topeka, KS, 1999. This book shows different ways to count to ten.

*   Hoban, Tana. *26 Letters and 99 Cents.* Mulberry Books, New York, 1995. The book provides an excellent visual representation of exchanging coin values.

At a Glance

Math Facts Strategies and Daily Practice and Problems

DPP items G, H, and J practice addition and subtraction math facts. Item I reviews measuring area.

Part 1. Coins (A1) (A3) (A5)

1. Give a student 100 pennies and have him or her count out 30¢.
2. Then, ask students to count to 30¢ using dimes.
3. The class discusses that it is faster to count to 30 by tens than by ones.
4. Students find the number of pennies, nickels, dimes, and quarters necessary to make 100¢.

Part 2. At the Fair (A1) (A2) (A3) (A5)

1. Students follow the rules on the *Arapaho County Fair* Transparency Master to find the number of dimes and nickels Tim and Jim each need to give to make $100.
2. Students record their solutions on the *Twins' Day at the County Fair* Activity Page.

Part 3. On the Bus (A1) (A2) (A3) (A4) (A5)

1. Students can use counters, calculators, and the *100 Chart* to complete the *Shuttle Bus #100* Activity Page.
2. Students discuss their strategies and record their solutions.

Homework

Assign the *Shuttle Bus #50* Homework Page as homework or as an assessment.

Assessment

Use Assessment Indicators A2 and A5 and the *Observational Assessment Record* to document students' abilities to use multiples of fives and tens to solve problems and to find the value of a collection of nickels, dimes, and quarters.

Extension

Have students skip count on the calculator by ones, fives, tens, and twenty-fives.

Connection

Read and discuss *Two Ways to Count to Ten* by Ruby Dee and *26 Letters and 99 Cents* by Tana Hoban.

Answer Key is on pages 60–61.

Notes

Name _____   Date _____

Nickels Money Master

Quarters Money Master

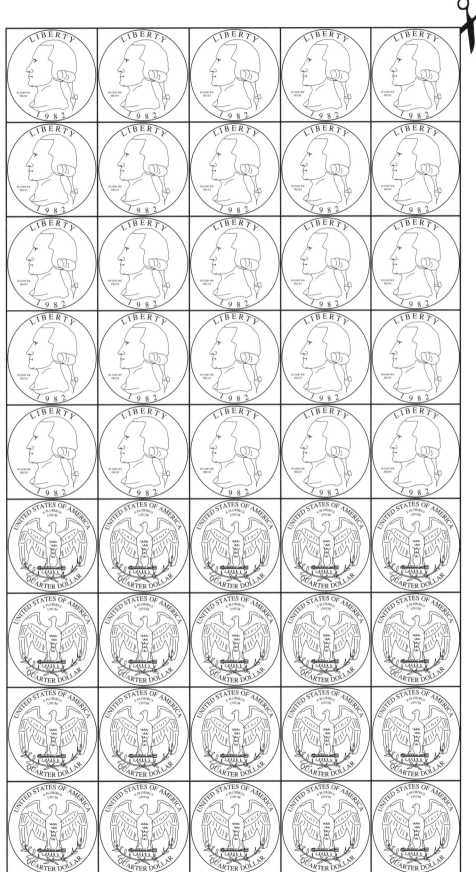

Arapaho County Fair

**Arapaho
County Fair**

Ferris Wheel....... $1.00

Balloon Toss...... $1.00

Target Range..... $1.00

Bumper Cars...... $1.00

Petting Zoo........$1.00

Gramps's Rules

1. Each child must give at least one coin for each ticket.
2. Use a different combination of coins for each ticket.
3. Keep a record of how the money is spent.
4. The coins the twins give must add up to $1.00.

Transparency Master

100 Chart

1	2	3	4	5	6	7	8	9	10
11	12	13	14	15	16	17	18	19	20
21	22	23	24	25	26	27	28	29	30
31	32	33	34	35	36	37	38	39	40
41	42	43	44	45	46	47	48	49	50
51	52	53	54	55	56	57	58	59	60
61	62	63	64	65	66	67	68	69	70
71	72	73	74	75	76	77	78	79	80
81	82	83	84	85	86	87	88	89	90
91	92	93	94	95	96	97	98	99	100

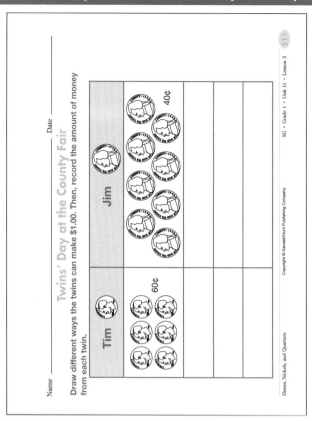

Student Guide - page 211

Student Guide (p. 211)

Twins' Day at the County Fair*

Answers will vary. Some possible combinations are:
1 dime and 18 nickels, 2 dimes and 16 nickels,
3 dimes and 14 nickels, 4 dimes and 12 nickels,
5 dimes and 10 nickels, 7 dimes and 6 nickels,
8 dimes and 4 nickels, and 9 dimes and 2 nickels.

Name _____ Date _____

Shuttle Bus #100

Shuttle bus #100 carries exactly 100 people each trip. It stops at three different parking lots. The people are picked up in groups of ten. The bus driver records the number of people picked up at each stop. Fill in the missing numbers on his chart. You can use beans on the number strip to help you.

| 10 | 10 | 10 | 10 | 10 | 10 | 10 | 10 | 10 | 10 |

Parking Lot 1		Parking Lot 2		Parking Lot 3	
20	+	50	+	_____	= 100
40	+	40	+	_____	= 100
10	+	60	+	_____	= 100
_____	+	20	+	60	= 100
60	+	_____	+	40	= 100
30	+	_____	+	40	= 100
50	+	40	+	_____	= 100
80	+	10	+	_____	= 100

SG • Grade 1 • Unit 11 • Lesson 3   Dimes, Nickels, and Quarters

Student Guide - page 212

Student Guide (p. 212)

Shuttle Bus #100*

$20 + 50 + 30 = 100$

$40 + 40 + 20 = 100$

$10 + 60 + 30 = 100$

$20 + 20 + 60 = 100$

$60 + 0 + 40 = 100$

$30 + 30 + 40 = 100$

$50 + 40 + 10 = 100$

$80 + 10 + 10 = 100$

*Answers and/or discussion are included in the Lesson Guide.

Student Guide (p. 213)

Shuttle Bus #50

$25 + 5 + 20 = 50$

$10 + 30 + 10 = 50$

$15 + 15 + 20 = 50$

$5 + 10 + 35 = 50$

$20 + 20 + 10 = 50$

$25 + 5 + 20 = 50$

$40 + 5 + 5 = 50$

$25 + 15 + 10 = 50$

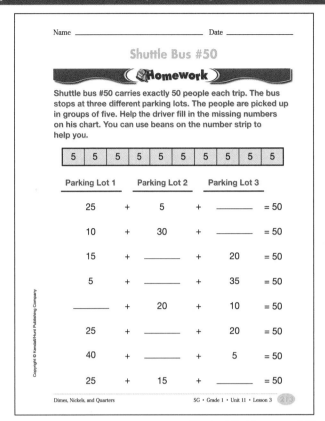

Name _____ Date _____

Shuttle Bus #50

Homework

Shuttle bus #50 carries exactly 50 people each trip. The bus stops at three different parking lots. The people are picked up in groups of five. Help the driver fill in the missing numbers on his chart. You can use beans on the number strip to help you.

| 5 | 5 | 5 | 5 | 5 | 5 | 5 | 5 | 5 | 5 |

Parking Lot 1		Parking Lot 2		Parking Lot 3	
25	+	5	+	_____	= 50
10	+	30	+	_____	= 50
15	+	_____	+	20	= 50
5	+	_____	+	35	= 50
_____	+	20	+	10	= 50
25	+	_____	+	20	= 50
40	+	_____	+	5	= 50
25	+	15	+	_____	= 50

Dimes, Nickels, and Quarters   SG • Grade 1 • Unit 11 • Lesson 3

Student Guide - page 213

Lesson 4

Arrow Dynamics

Lesson Overview

Estimated Class Sessions

1

Students develop their knowledge of number relationships by playing the game *Arrow Dynamics* on a *100 Chart*. After each player makes a move on the chart, he or she writes a number sentence to describe the move. The player who gets closest to 100 wins the game.

Key Content

- Using a *100 Chart* to represent numbers.
- Using a *100 Chart* to solve problems.
- Writing number sentences for addition and subtraction situations.

Math Facts Strategies

DPP items K and L provide addition math facts practice.

Homework

1. *The Who Is Winning?* Activity Page can be used as homework.
2. Have students play *Arrow Dynamics* at home. They will need a *100 Chart* and one copy each of the *Arrow Dynamics Game Board* and *Arrow Dynamics Record Sheet* as well as a spinner (or a paper clip and pencil).

Assessment

1. Assign the *Follow the Arrows* Assessment Page after playing a few games of *Arrow Dynamics*.
2. Use DPP item L, Assessment Indicator A7, and the *Observational Assessment Record* to document students' abilities to solve the math facts in Group A. Note which strategies students use.

Materials List

Supplies and Copies

Student	Teacher
Supplies for Each Student Pair • spinner or paper clip and pencil • 2 different-colored game markers	**Supplies**
Copies • extra copies of *100 Chart* as needed (*Unit Resource Guide* Page 59)	**Copies/Transparencies** • 1 transparency of *Arrow Dynamics Game Board,* optional (*Student Guide* Page 215) • 1 transparency of *100 Chart,* optional (*Student Guide* Page 217)

All blackline masters including assessment, transparency, and DPP masters are also on the Teacher Resource CD.

Student Books
Arrow Dynamics Game Board (*Student Guide* Page 215)
100 Chart (*Student Guide* Page 217)
Arrow Dynammics Record Sheet (*Student Guide* Pages 219–220)
Who Is Winning? (*Student Guide* Page 221)
Follow the Arrows (*Student Guide* Page 223)

Daily Practice and Problems
DPP items K–L (*Unit Resource Guide* Page 22)

Assessment Tools
Observational Assessment Record (*Unit Resource Guide* Pages 13–14)

Suggestions for using the DPPs are on pages 66–67.

K. Pennies and Dimes Again

(URG p. 22)

1. Karen has 3 pennies. Sheila has 1 penny. How much change do they have altogether?
2. Nolan has 3 dimes. Scott has 1 dime. How much change do the boys have altogether?

L. Addition Facts 3 (URG p. 22)

A. $0 + 1 =$ ☐   B. $1 + 1 =$ ☐

C. $1 + 3 =$ ☐   D. $2 + 1 =$ ☐

Explain how you solved C.

Students play the game *Arrow Dynamics* in pairs. Each student should have the *Arrow Dynamics Game Board* Game Page, the *100 Chart* Activity Page, and the *Arrow Dynamics Record Sheet* Game Page. Explain that each player begins by placing his or her marker on the "45" box of the *100 Chart*. Players take turns spinning to find out which direction to move on the *100 Chart*. A player whose spinner lands on an arrow pointing left moves one space in that direction. For this reason, students should keep their spinners and *100 Charts* facing the same direction for the entire game. The winner is the player who is closest to the number 100 after seven spins.

Demonstrate how to spin and move using the transparencies of the *Arrow Dynamics Game Board* and the *100 Chart*. If a player cannot move in the direction of the arrow because the marker is at an outer edge of the *100 Chart,* she or he should spin again. Each player should say a number sentence to describe her or his move after each turn and record

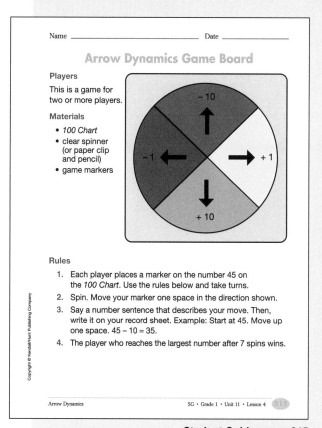

Name _____ Date _____

Arrow Dynamics Game Board

Players

This is a game for two or more players.

Materials

- *100 Chart*
- clear spinner (or paper clip and pencil)
- game markers

Rules

1. Each player places a marker on the number 45 on the *100 Chart*. Use the rules below and take turns.
2. Spin. Move your marker one space in the direction shown.
3. Say a number sentence that describes your move. Then, write it on your record sheet. Example: Start at 45. Move up one space. 45 − 10 = 35.
4. The player who reaches the largest number after 7 spins wins.

Arrow Dynamics   SG • Grade 1 • Unit 11 • Lesson 4   215

Student Guide - page 215

Name _____ Date _____

100 Chart

1	2	3	4	5	6	7	8	9	10
11	12	13	14	15	16	17	18	19	20
21	22	23	24	25	26	27	28	29	30
31	32	33	34	35	36	37	38	39	40
41	42	43	44	45	46	47	48	49	50
51	52	53	54	55	56	57	58	59	60
61	62	63	64	65	66	67	68	69	70
71	72	73	74	75	76	77	78	79	80
81	82	83	84	85	86	87	88	89	90
91	92	93	94	95	96	97	98	99	100

Arrow Dynamics   SG • Grade 1 • Unit 11 • Lesson 4   217

Student Guide - page 217

Name _____ Date _____

Arrow Dynamics Record Sheet 1

Write a number sentence to describe each move.

Player 1	Player 2

Arrow Dynamics   SG • Grade 1 • Unit 11 • Lesson 4   219

Student Guide - page 219

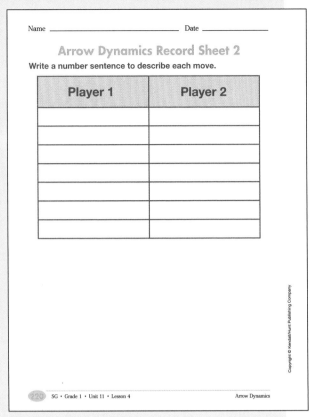

Student Guide - page 220

it on the *Arrow Dynamics Record Sheet*. Demonstrate how to do this on the overhead, writing the number sentence on the board for students to refer to.

Example: the game marker is on 45, you spin a left arrow, you move your marker one space to the left. You are now on 44. A number sentence for this is $45 - 1 = 44$. If you moved up one space, it would be $45 - 10 = 35$. If you moved to the right one space, it would be $45 + 1 = 46$. If you moved down one space, it would be $45 + 10 = 55$.

The *Who Is Winning?* Activity Page can be used as either a pre-game demonstration or an after-game practice of adding and subtracting on the *100 Chart*. Students will need their *100 Chart* to answer questions.

Math Facts Strategies

DPP item K practices math facts strategies for addition.

Homework and Practice

* The *Who Is Winning?* Activity Page can be used as homework after students have played the game *Arrow Dynamics*. Students will need a *100 Chart*.

* Have students take the game *Arrow Dynamics* home to play with family members. They will need a *100 Chart* and one copy each of the *Arrow Dynamics Game Board* and *Arrow Dynamics Record Sheet* as well as a spinner (or a paper clip and pencil).

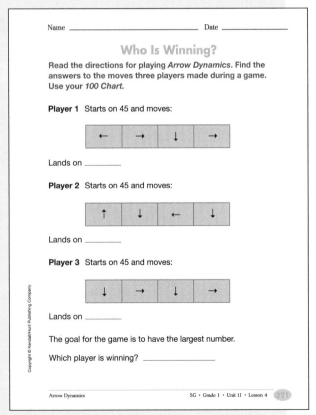

Student Guide - page 221 *(Answers on p. 69)*

- Assign the *Follow the Arrows* Assessment Page to evaluate students' understanding of the activity's concepts. Notice that the starting point varies from the usual 45. Students need a *100 Chart* to complete the activity.

- Use DPP item L to assess the addition math facts in Group A. (Items L and N together assess all the facts in Group A.) These facts can be solved by counting on. Use the *Observational Assessment Record* to record students' progress toward fluency with these facts and which math facts strategies students use. For more information on the distribution and assessment of the math facts, see the Background and Daily Practice and Problems Guide for this unit.

Extension

- A variation of *Arrow Dynamics* is *Going to Extremes*. The game is played the same way as *Arrow Dynamics* except that a winner is a player who gets closest to either 0 or 100. There could be two winners when playing this way.

- Another variation is to let students choose their own starting numbers and ending numbers.

Name _____ Date _____

Follow the Arrows

Here are some moves in an *Arrow Dynamics* game. Write a number sentence to describe each move. Use your *100 Chart*.

1. Start on 45. Move [→]. Land on _____

   Number Sentence: _____

2. Start on 55. Move [↓]. Land on _____

   Number Sentence: _____

3. Start on 58. Move [←]. Land on _____

   Number Sentence: _____

4. Start on 92. Move [↑ ↑]. Land on _____

   Number Sentence: _____

5. Start on 12. Move [← ↑]. Land on _____

   Number Sentence: _____

Arrow Dynamics   SG • Grade 1 • Unit 11 • Lesson 4   223

Student Guide - page 223 *(Answers on p. 69)*

Math Facts Strategies and Daily Practice and Problems (A7)

DPP items K and L practice addition math facts.

Teaching the Activity (A4)

1. Assign students to partners and tell them to place their game markers on the number 45 on their own *100 Chart.* Demonstrate with a transparency of the *100 Chart.*

2. Players take turns spinning on their *Arrow Dynamics Game Board* to see what direction they will move their markers. Demonstrate playing the game with a transparency of the *Arrow Dynamics Game Board.*

3. After moving one space in the direction of the arrow, players write a number sentence that reflects the move on their *Arrow Dynamics Record Sheet.* Write examples on the board.

4. Use the *Who Is Winning?* Activity Page as either a pre-game warm-up or an after-game review. Students need *100 Charts* to answer the questions.

Homework

1. The *Who Is Winning?* Activity Page can be used as homework.

2. Have students play *Arrow Dynamics* at home. They will need a *100 Chart* and one copy each of the *Arrow Dynamics Game Board* and *Arrow Dynamics Record Sheet* as well as a spinner (or a paper clip and pencil).

Assessment

1. Assign the *Follow the Arrows* Assessment Page after playing a few games of *Arrow Dynamics.*

2. Use DPP item L, Assessment Indicator A7, and the *Observational Assessment Record* to document students' abilities to solve the math facts in Group A. Note which strategies students use.

Extension

1. Play *Going to Extremes* with students.

2. Play a variation of the game; let students choose their own starting number.

Answer Key is on page 69.

Notes:

Student Guide (p. 221)

Who Is Winning?
56, 54, 67; Player 3

Name _____ **Date** _____

Who Is Winning?
Read the directions for playing *Arrow Dynamics*. Find the answers to the moves three players made during a game. Use your *100 Chart*.

Player 1 Starts on 45 and moves:

| ← | → | ↓ | → |

Lands on _____

Player 2 Starts on 45 and moves:

| ↑ | ↓ | ← | ↓ |

Lands on _____

Player 3 Starts on 45 and moves:

| ↓ | → | ↓ | → |

Lands on _____

The goal for the game is to have the largest number.

Which player is winning? _____

Arrow Dynamics   SG • Grade 1 • Unit 11 • Lesson 4   221

Student Guide - page 221

Student Guide (p. 223)

Follow the Arrows
1. 46; 45 + 1 = 46
2. 65; 55 + 10 = 65
3. 57; 58 − 1 = 57
4. 72; 92 − 10 − 10 = 72
5. 1; 12 − 1 − 10 = 1

Name _____ **Date** _____

Follow the Arrows
Here are some moves in an *Arrow Dynamics* game. Write a number sentence to describe each move. Use your *100 Chart*.

1. Start on 45. Move [→]. Land on _____
Number Sentence: _____

2. Start on 55. Move [↓]. Land on _____
Number Sentence: _____

3. Start on 58. Move [←]. Land on _____
Number Sentence: _____

4. Start on 92. Move [↑][↑]. Land on _____
Number Sentence: _____

5. Start on 12. Move [←][↑]. Land on _____
Number Sentence: _____

Arrow Dynamics   SG • Grade 1 • Unit 11 • Lesson 4   223

Student Guide - page 223

Lesson 5

How Long Is 100?

Lesson Overview

Estimated Class Sessions

1

Students use seconds and minutes to develop number sense for 100. They use a calculator to find how high they can count by ones in 100 seconds. Then, they predict and test how many X marks they can make in 100 seconds. The activity concludes with students answering questions about a class data table showing the results of their experiment.

Key Content

- Using seconds and minutes.
- Developing number sense for 100.
- Placing numbers into intervals.
- Interpreting data in a table.

Math Facts Strategies

DPP item M reviews the value of dimes. DPP item N provides addition math facts practice.

Assessment

Use DPP item N, Assessment Indicator A7, and the *Observational Assessment Record* to document students' use of math facts strategies for the Group A addition facts.

Materials List

Supplies and Copies

Student	Teacher
Supplies for Each Student • calculator	**Supplies**
Copies	**Copies/Transparencies** • 1 transparency of *100 Seconds Class Data Table* (*Unit Resource Guide* Page 75)

All blackline masters including assessment, transparency, and DPP masters are also on the Teacher Resource CD.

Student Books
100 Seconds (*Student Guide* Page 225)

Daily Practice and Problems
DPP items M–N (*Unit Resource Guide* Page 23)

Assessment Tools
Observational Assessment Record (*Unit Resource Guide* Pages 13–14)

Daily Practice and Problems

Suggestions for using the DPPs are on page 73.

M. How Many Dimes? (URG p. 23)

Julie arranged some dimes into two piles.
Then, she wrote the following number sentence:
20 cents + 30 cents = 50 cents.

1. How many dimes are in each of Julie's piles?
2. How many dimes does she have in all?
3. How much are all the dimes worth?

N. Addition Facts 4 (URG p. 23)

A. $0 + 2 =$ ☐

B. $2 + 4 =$ ☐

C. $2 + 2 =$ ☐

D. $3 + 2 =$ ☐

E. $2 + 1 =$ ☐

Explain how you solved D.

TIMS Tip

Have students work in pairs to come up with answers before you discuss each question as a group.

Teaching the Activity

Begin a discussion of time units by asking students how long in time 100 is. Some may ask, "100 what?" Discuss the fact that to say how long 100 is, we need to know what unit of time we are dealing with—seconds, minutes, hours, days, or something even longer. Have students close their eyes for 100 seconds to give them a sense of the duration. Use questions like those that follow to guide a class discussion about units of time.

100 Seconds

- *What can you do in 100 seconds? Can you run around the school building or put on your coat, hat, boots, and gloves?*
- *Does 100 seconds seem like a (long, short) time?*

100 Minutes

- *How long is 100 minutes?*
- *What were we doing 100 minutes ago?*
- *What will we be doing 100 minutes from now?*
- *Does 100 minutes seem like a (long, short) time?*

Give students a real sense of what they can accomplish in 100 seconds. Each student should have a calculator. Tell them to press

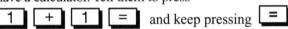 and keep pressing

for 100 seconds. Students read their calculator window to see how high they counted by ones in 100 seconds.

Next, students will make as many X marks as they can on the *100 Seconds* Activity Page while you time them for 100 seconds. Explain that they should draw one X mark in each box. Make sure students understand that this is not a race and that X marks do not have to be drawn exactly from corner to corner.

Before they begin, ask:

- *Predict how many X marks you can draw in 100 seconds.*

Have students base their prediction on a sample. Have students draw as many X marks as they can in 10 seconds, then use their data to make their prediction for 100 seconds. Each student should record his or her prediction on the *100 Seconds* Activity Page and compare it with the actual number when finished.

Name _____ Date _____

100 Seconds

Draw one X in each box. How many Xs do you think you can draw in 100 seconds? Try it for 10 seconds and then make a prediction.

How many Xs did you draw in 10 seconds?

_____

How many Xs do you think you could draw in 100 seconds?

_____

Try it. How many Xs did you draw in 100 seconds?

_____

Look at your prediction. Were you close? Why or why not?

_____

_____

_____

How Long Is 100?   SG • Grade 1 • Unit 11 • Lesson 5   225

Student Guide - page 225 *(Answers on p. 76)*

TIMS Tip

Students can test their predictions for 100 seconds in a different color pen or on *Centimeter Grid Paper* to avoid having to count the number of X marks in both trials.

Display the *100 Seconds Class Data Table*
Transparency Master and have students tell you where
to record their number of X marks on the table.

Intervals	Actual Numbers	Total Number
0 – 10		0
11 – 20	12, 17, 14, 16, 18, 11	6
21 – 30	26, 27, 27, 23, 22, 29, 30	7
31 – 40		

Figure 3: *A sample class data table*

Then, use the following questions or similar ones to
discuss the table:

- *What is the greatest number of X marks made in
  100 seconds?*

- *What is the smallest number of X marks made in
  100 seconds?*

- *What is the range (lowest to highest) of X marks
  made in 100 seconds?*

- *What is the interval where most students ended?
  What is the most common interval?*

- *If I made a graph of these data, which interval
  would have the tallest bar?*

Math Facts Strategies

DPP item M practices adding one-digit numbers and
then generalizes to adding tens.

Assessment

Use DPP item N to assess the math facts in Group A.
(Items L and N together assess all the facts in Group
A.) Students can count on to solve these facts. Use
the *Observational Assessment Record* to document
students' progress with these facts and which strategies students use.

At a Glance

Math Facts Strategies and Daily Practice and Problems (A7)

DPP item M reviews the value of dimes. DPP item N practices addition math facts.

Teaching the Activity (A1)

1. Students discuss how long 100 is based on its units.
2. Students close their eyes for 100 seconds.
3. Students use a calculator to see how high they can count by ones in 100 seconds.
4. Students predict how many X marks they can draw in 100 seconds on the *100 Seconds* Activity Page.
5. Students record their predictions and test them.
6. Students tell the actual number of X marks made. Record scores on a transparency of the *100 Seconds Class Data Table.*
7. Students analyze and discuss the results in the class data table.

Assessment

Use DPP item N, Assessment Indicator A7, and the *Observational Assessment Record* to document students' use of math facts strategies for the Group A addition facts.

Answer Key is on page 76.

Notes:

100 Seconds Class Data Table

Intervals	Actual Numbers	Total Number
0 – 10		
11 – 20		
21 – 30		
31 – 40		
41 – 50		
51 – 60		
61 – 70		
71 – 80		
81 – 90		
91 – 100		
101 – 110		
111 – 120		
121 – 130		
131 – 140		
141 – 150		
151 – 160		
161 – 170		
171 – 180		

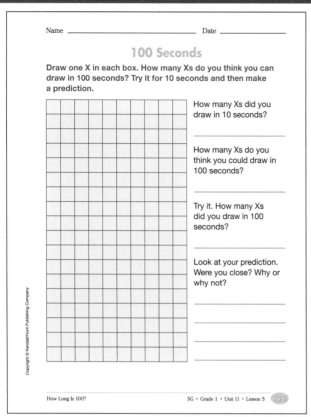

Student Guide - page 225

Student Guide (p. 225)

100 Seconds

Answers will vary.*

*Answers and/or discussion are included in the Lesson Guide.

Lesson 6

Weather 2: Winter Skies

Lesson Overview

Estimated Class Sessions

1

In this lab, students observe and record daily weather conditions for a winter month. This lab is an extension of *Weather 1: Eye on the Sky.* We recommend scheduling these labs in October and February. The directions focus on these months. However, if this is not possible, try to provide a gap of three months between the first and second lab.

This lab is an ongoing activity. Students discuss their predictions and prepare to record their observations in an introductory lesson at the beginning of the month. Throughout the month, students classify and record sky conditions. In two final sessions at the end of the month, students graph the data they have collected to analyze and discuss it. Students compare and contrast their graphs of the February weather conditions with those from October. This lab, together with its counterpart, *Weather 1: Eye on the Sky,* provides a setting for two important scientific skills:

- comparing sets of data in which a controlled variable has been changed; and
- evaluating the reliability of a sample in making predictions.

Key Content

- Translating between different representations of numbers (tallies and symbols).
- Collecting, organizing, graphing, and analyzing data and recording data.
- Making and interpreting bar graphs.
- Comparing sets of data in which one variable has been changed.

- Using patterns in data to make predictions and solve problems.
- Translating between graphs and real-world events.
- Connecting mathematics and science to real-world situations: recording weather data.
- Using a calendar to measure the passage of time.

Homework

Use the *Weekend Weather* Blackline Master for homework. Because the time of day must remain constant, students should make their observation times on the blank clock the same as the class time.

Assessment

1. Use the *Winter Weather* Assessment Page.
2. Use Assessment Indicator A6 and the *Observational Assessment Record* to document students' abilities to use the calendar to measure the passage of time.

Curriculum Sequence

Before This Unit

Time and Calendar Work

In Grade 1 Unit 2 Lesson 6 students began work with time concepts using the calendar in *Weather 1*. Students also used the calendar to solve problems throughout the Daily Practice and Problems.

Materials List

Supplies and Copies

Student	Teacher
Supplies for Each Student	**Supplies**
Copies • 1 copy of *Weekend Weather* per student each weekend, optional (*Unit Resource Guide* Page 88)	**Copies/Transparencies** • 1 transparency of *Weather 2 Graph* (*Student Guide* Page 231) • 1 transparency of *Weather 1 Graph* from Unit 2 Lesson 6 • 1 transparency of *Weather Data* (*Student Guide* Page 235)

All blackline masters including assessment, transparency, and DPP masters are also on the Teacher Resource CD.

Student Books

Daily Practice and Problems

Assessment Tools

Daily Practice and Problems

Suggestions for using the DPPs are on page 85.

O. Back at the Circus (URG p. 24)

Twenty-five acrobats were in the ring. Five more joined them. How many acrobats are in the ring now?

P. Sharing Peanuts (URG p. 24)

Jane, her sister, and father shared a bag of peanuts. There were 17 peanuts in the bag. How many peanuts should each person get if they share the peanuts fairly?

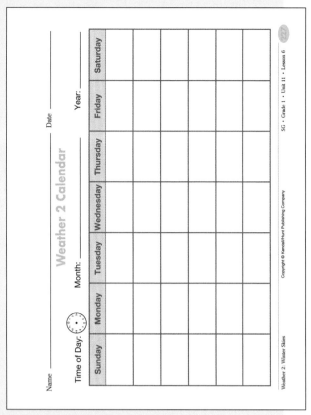

Student Guide - page 227 *(Answers on p. 89)*

Journal Prompt

Which month has more sunny days, October or February? How can you find out?

Content Note

Variables. The idea of controlled, or fixed, variables in an investigation is a very important one. When we compare sets of data, it is essential that only one variable change among the sets. If we observe differences in data and only one variable has changed, then we can say with some certainty that the changed variable is the source of the data differences. In this lab, students repeat the *Weather 1: Eye on the Sky* lab, keeping the variables time of day and location constant and changing only the time of year variable.

TIMS Tip

Refer to the TIMS Tutor: *The TIMS Laboratory Method* in the *Teacher Implementation Guide* for more information about this process.

Teaching the Lab

This investigation should start on the first school day of the month and continue through the last day of the month. Each day, students will observe and record their data for the variable Type of Sky—sunny, partly sunny, or cloudy—on the *Weather 2 Calendar* Lab Page. Type of Sky is the same variable students studied in the *Weather 1: Eye on the Sky* lab during October. Students will keep the variables time of day and location the same as they were in *Weather 1: Eye on the Sky*. At the end of the month, students will compare the graphs for the two months. We recommend February and October. Although there are 31 days in October and 28 or 29 days in February, a difference of two or three days should not significantly affect the shape of the graph. During the discussion of the graphs, students evaluate a sample's reliability for making predictions.

Part 1 Launching the Investigation

Using questions like these, ask students how skies this month might compare to skies in October.

- *Are October skies about as (sunny, cloudy) as the skies this month?*

- *In which month would you expect a greater number of cloudy days—a month in autumn or a month in winter?*

- *Compared to a winter month, does an autumn month have (more, about the same number of, or fewer) sunny days?*

Students' responses are likely to be disparate and will vary depending on your geographic location. Tally the responses on the chalkboard. Help students recognize that they can find the answer if they compare the data they collected in October with the data for the current month. Note students' predictions to refer to when finishing this lab at the end of the month.

Explain that scientists modify experiments to answer specific questions. Then, model this aspect of the scientific process. Remind students of the *Weather 1: Eye on the Sky* lab they completed in October. Suggest that they will repeat the *Weather 1: Eye on the Sky* lab. They will collect a second set of data, keeping the variables time of day and location the same and changing only the variable time of year.

Part 2 Drawing the Picture

To determine which month, October or February, has more sunny days, more cloudy days, and more partly sunny days, students can use the TIMS Laboratory Method.

Students can fill in all the dates on the *Weather 2 Calendar* Lab Page now, or they can fill in each date as they record their daily observation. Discuss the type of sky descriptions they used during *Weather 1: Eye on the Sky.* Reviewing students' perceptions of *sunny, partly sunny,* and *cloudy* will facilitate data collecting and recording. Suggest that they draw pictures of sunny, partly sunny, and cloudy skies in the first column of the *Weather 2 Data Table* Lab Page. Ask:

* *Why is it important to collect the data at the same time each day?* (To be able to compare fall days to winter days, we need to keep the time of day the same. Students might recall times when the day started as sunny and changed to cloudy, for example. Since we want to keep the time of day as it was in *Weather 1,* students should record on the blank clock of *Weather 2 Calendar* the same time as they used on their October calendar.)

After you feel confident that students understand how they will collect, record, and compare the data, ask students to draw pictures of the investigation on the *Weather 2 Picture* Lab Page.

Figure 4 shows an example of student work.

Figure 4: *Sample student picture of the* Weather 2: Winter Skies *lab*

Note that in Figure 4 the student has identified time of day as the controlled variable and type of sky as the variable to be measured. The student has also shown that the time of year is February. The initial discussion and picture drawing might take about one session.

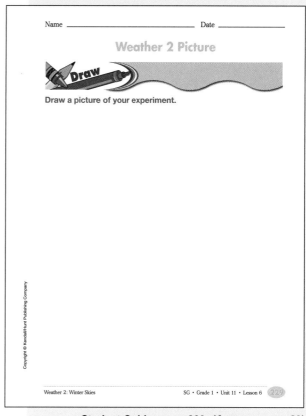

Student Guide - page 229 *(Answers on p. 89)*

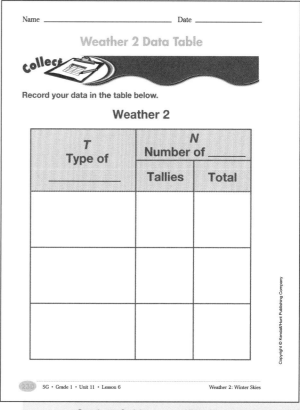

Student Guide - page 230 *(Answers on p. 90)*

Ask two or three students to volunteer to be "weather watchers" each week. The weather watchers can remind students when to observe the type of sky. This will help ensure that students make observations even within a busy schedule. The weather watchers can also be responsible for reporting the weather on any holidays.

Part 3 Collecting and Organizing the Data

Each day during February, students check the sky and agree on the type of sky—sunny, partly sunny, or cloudy. Students record data in two places. First, they use the *Weather 2 Calendar* Lab Page. Have students draw the appropriate value for the type of sky on the appropriate day on the calendar. Be certain students use the same drawings they made in the data table. Second, students place one tally mark in the corresponding row of the *Weather 2 Data Table* Lab Page.

After one week of data collection, ask students:

- *Can you use your data to predict the type of sky for the rest of the month?*

Encourage students to suggest reasons for and against making a prediction. If they choose to make a prediction, have them decide how to record and then check their prediction. This is also a good time to prepare students to collect data at home for the weekend weather. (See the Homework and Practice section of Suggestions for Teaching the Lesson.)

Part 4 Graphing the Data

At the end of February, the process of graphing and analyzing the data begins. Have students transfer their data to the graph on the *Weather 2 Graph* Lab Page. Students will need to complete numbering and labeling the axes. Review the idea that the table and the graph show the same information in different ways.

After students complete the graph, ask them to share some of the information it tells them about the data. You may ask:

- *Which type of sky has the tallest bar on the graph? What does that tell you about that type of sky?* (Responses should match the graph—i.e., the type of sky with the tallest bar is the type of sky students observed most often.)

- *Which type of sky has the shortest bar on the graph? What does that tell you about that type of sky?* (Responses should match the graph—i.e., the type of sky with the shortest bar is the type of sky students observed least often.)

- *Did you see one type of sky on more than half the days in the month?* (Strategies might include folding the calendar in half, counting out 28 cubes and making two equally tall towers, crossing off days starting with the first and last days and working towards the middle.)

Part 5 Exploring the Data

After a thorough class discussion about the data, students should complete the questions on the *Thinking about Winter Skies* Lab Page individually or with a partner.

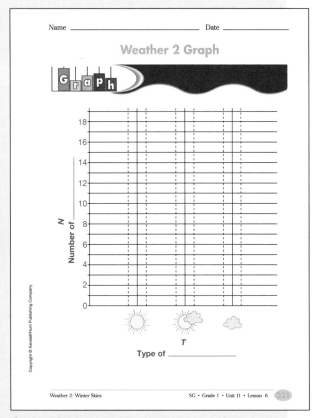

Student Guide - page 231 *(Answers on p. 90)*

Suggest to students that they also explore the data by finding a story in the graph. Figure 5 shows a sample graph. A story for this graph could be: *"In February, 4 days were sunny; 10 days were sunny and cloudy; and 14 days were cloudy. Half of the days in February were cloudy and lots of the days were sunny part of the time."*

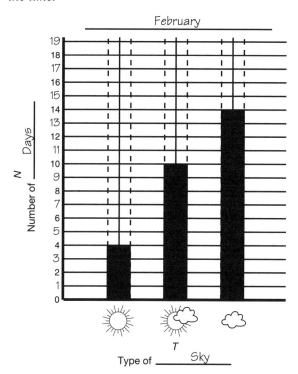

Figure 5: *Sample graph*

Place a transparency of the completed October graph from *Weather 1* on the overhead projector and model some ways to tell the story of a graph.

- *What are some of the important things you see when you look at the graph?*

Give students the opportunity to share their ideas. Then, ask students to tell the story of the *Weather 2 Graph* they just completed. After students complete a story for the *Weather 2 Graph,* encourage them to compare their *Weather 2 Graph* for February with their *Weather 1 Graph* for October.

Some students may eagerly point out that the number of days in the two months was not the same. Acknowledge this difference; then, direct students' attention to the shape of the data on the graph, that is, remind them of each graph's story. The shape of the data determines the story. A difference of two or three days' data will probably not affect how two stories compare.

Suggest that each student work with a partner to decide how the stories of the *Weather 1* and *2 Graphs* (autumn and winter) compare. After students describe

---

Name _____ Date _____

Thinking about Winter Skies

Explore

1. Which type of sky did you see *most* often?
   _____

2. Which type of sky did you see *least* often?
   _____

3. How many sunny *and* partly sunny skies were there in all?
   _____

4. Were there more cloudy skies or more sunny skies?
   _____

5. How many days are there in half of this winter month?
   _____

6. A. Was any type of sky seen on more than half the days
   in the month? _____

   B. Which type of sky was it? _____

SG • Grade 1 • Unit 11 • Lesson 6   Weather 2: Winter Skies

Student Guide - page 232 (Answers on p. 91)

Name _____ Date _____

Comparing Fall and Winter Skies

Explore

Record your data for each month's weather in the data table.

T Type of Sky _____	N Number of Days	
	month	month
☀		
⛅		
☁		

1. A. Which month had more sunny days? _____

   B. How many more? _____

   C. Is this a big difference or a small difference?
   _____

Weather 2: Winter Skies   SG • Grade 1 • Unit 11 • Lesson 6

Student Guide - page 233 (Answers on p. 91)

2. A. Which month had more partly sunny days?

    _____

    B. How many more? _____
    C. Is this a big difference or a small difference?

    _____

3. A. Which month had more cloudy days? _____
    B. How many more? _____
    C. Is this a big difference or a small difference?

    _____

4. When would you expect more cloudy days—an autumn
    month or a winter month?

    _____

    How can you use the data to answer this question?

    _____
    _____
    _____

Student Guide - page 234 *(Answers on p. 91)*

Weather Data

September's Weather		October's Weather	
T Type of Day	**N** Number of Days	**T** Type of Day	**N** Number of Days
☀	16	☀	13
⛅	5	⛅	14
☁	9	☁	4

November's Weather		December's Weather	
T Type of Day	**N** Number of Days	**T** Type of Day	**N** Number of Days
☀	7	☀	3
⛅	8	⛅	11
☁	15	☁	17

Student Guide - page 235

to their partners how the stories are alike and different, invite them to share their ideas with the entire class.

Bring the lab to a close by using the *Comparing Fall and Winter Skies* Lab Pages. Students will need to add to the data table the names of the two months they used. To help students compare the two months, review the discussion the class had in Part 1 Launching the Investigation and refer to the predictions students made. Ask the following questions again. Allow students to revise their initial answers based on their collected data. If you had students make or review predictions after the first week of data collection, compare these predictions with the actual results as well.

*   *Were October skies about as (sunny, cloudy) as February skies?*

*   *Which month had a greater number of cloudy days—the autumn month or the winter month?*

*   *Compared to the winter month, did the autumn month have (more, about the same number of, or fewer) sunny days?* (Students should be able to use data to support their answers.)

When students have demonstrated their ability to tell the story of the graphs, present student pairs with the *Weather Data* and *Weather Problems* Lab Pages. The *Weather Problems* prompt students to use the information from data tables on the *Weather Data* page to answer questions. Help students by discussing the tools—*100 Chart,* counters, counting on—that they have available to help them solve the problems. Encourage student pairs to decide whether to write or draw their solution paths. After students have worked on these questions independently, allow time for them to share the thinking they used to solve the problems. Explore several ways to find the total of sunny days recorded on the *Weather Data* Lab Page. See **Question 4** on the *Weather Problems* Lab Pages.

Homework and Practice

*   Have students record the sky conditions during the weekends on the *Weekend Weather* Blackline Master. Because the time of day must remain constant, students should indicate when to make their observations—the same as the class time— on the blank clock. Students may report different conditions, particularly if a child took a trip. Use the situation to lead a discussion of whether sky conditions are the same everywhere.

*   Students can use the data on the *Weather Data* Lab Page to write their own problems. Suggest that students be able to describe at least two ways

to solve any problem they write. As you display a transparency of the page, spark students' thinking with questions such as these:

- *What was the total number of partly sunny days in the four months?*
- *Which type of sky was observed most often in the four months?*
- *How many more sunny days were in September and October than were in November and December?*

  Pool students' problems. Allow student pairs to draw one or two problems from the pool and to work together to find other ways to find the solutions.

- DPP item O is an addition word problem. Item P reviews fair shares and leftovers.

Assessment

- The *Winter Weather* Assessment Page asks students to write a story for two graphs of December skies. One graph represents data collected in Tucson, Arizona, and the other data collected in Chicago, Illinois. This page will help you assess students' abilities to interpret bar graphs.

- Use the *Observational Assessment Record* to note if students can use a calendar to measure the passage of time.

Name _____ Date _____

Weather Problems

Michael and Bianca are doing a science project. They compared the data they collected for four months. They recorded their data on the *Weather Data* Activity Page. Use this data to answer these questions.

1. How many sunny days did they record for December and November? _____

   Write a number sentence to show how you found the answer.

   _____

2. How many more cloudy days were there in September than in October? _____

   Write a number sentence to show how you found the answer.

   _____

3. How many days were cloudy in September and October?

   _____

   Write a number sentence to show how you found the answer.

   _____

Weather 2: Winter Skies   SG • Grade 1 • Unit 11 • Lesson 6

Student Guide - page 237 *(Answers on p. 92)*

Name _____ Date _____

4. They found there were 39 sunny days in the four months.

   Is their total correct? _____

   How did you decide?

   _____
   _____
   _____

   What is another way to find the total number of sunny days?

   _____
   _____
   _____
   _____

   Think of other problems you can ask about these data tables. Write the problems in your journal.

SG • Grade 1 • Unit 11 • Lesson 6   Weather 2: Winter Skies

Student Guide - page 238 *(Answers on p. 92)*

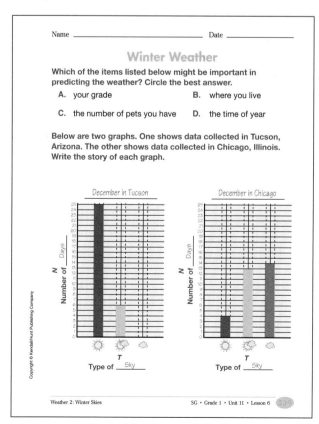

Name _____ Date _____

Winter Weather

Which of the items listed below might be important in predicting the weather? Circle the best answer.

A. your grade   B. where you live

C. the number of pets you have   D. the time of year

Below are two graphs. One shows data collected in Tucson, Arizona. The other shows data collected in Chicago, Illinois. Write the story of each graph.

Weather 2: Winter Skies   SG • Grade 1 • Unit 11 • Lesson 6

Student Guide - page 239 *(Answers on p. 93)*

- The weather data collection and comparison provides a good setting to think about when to use samples to predict. As students compare data from fall and winter, challenge them with such questions as:

  - *If you were a weather forecaster, which graph*—Weather 1 *(autumn) or* Weather 2 *(winter)—would you use to predict next October's skies? Why?* (Students are likely to say that they would use the October graph because all Octobers are much the same.)

  - *Suppose you used your* Weather 2 Graph *to predict next February's skies. Could you tell exactly how many sunny days there would be?* (Student responses should indicate that although they can tell exactly how many sunny days there were this year, they wouldn't know exactly how many there would be next year. The best they could do is to tell *about* how many there would be.)

- The Adventure Book *It's Sunny in Arizona* ties in well with this lab.

Literature Connection

Gibbons, Gail. *Weather Forecasting*. Aladdin Books, New York, 1993.

Estimated Class Sessions

1

At a Glance

Math Facts Strategies and Daily Practice and Problems

DPP item O provides addition practice. Item P provides practice with partitioning numbers into parts.

Part 1. Launching the Investigation

1. On the first of the month, students predict how the weather in February might compare with their observations of the weather in October.

2. Students develop a plan to repeat the lab *Weather 1: Eye on the Sky* done in October to collect similar data for February weather.

Part 2. Drawing the Picture (A6)

1. Students prepare the *Weather 2 Calendar* Lab Page to use through the month and review how they will collect, record, and compare the data.

2. Students draw pictures of the investigation on the *Weather 2 Picture* Lab Page to show how they will carry out the investigation.

At a Glance

Part 3. Collecting and Organizing the Data (A6)

1. Each day during February, students check the sky and record their observations on the *Weather 2 Calendar* Lab Page and tally their findings on the *Weather 2 Data Table* Lab Page.
2. After collecting data for one week, students use their data to revise or confirm their original predictions.
3. As homework, students record the sky conditions for each day of the weekend.

Part 4. Graphing the Data

1. At the end of the month, students transfer their data to the graph on the *Weather 2 Graph* Lab Page.
2. Students discuss what the graph tells them about the data.

Part 5. Exploring the Data

1. Students complete the *Thinking about Winter Skies* Activity Page.
2. Students develop stories about their graphs.
3. Students compare the story that the *Weather 2 Graph* for February tells about the weather with that of the *Weather 1 Graph* for October.
4. Students complete the *Comparing Fall and Winter Skies* Lab Pages.
5. Students demonstrate their abilities to use the data tables to solve problems using the *Weather Data* and *Weather Problems* Lab Pages.
6. Have students use the data on the *Weather Data* Lab Page to write their own problems. Pool students' problems. Allow student pairs to draw one or two problems from the pool and to work together to find other solutions.

Homework

Use the *Weekend Weather* Blackline Master for homework. Because the time of day must remain constant, students should make their observation times on the blank clock the same as the class time.

Assessment

1. Use the *Winter Weather* Assessment Page.
2. Use Assessment Indicator A6 and the *Observational Assessment Record* to document students' abilities to use the calendar to measure the passage of time.

Extension

1. Use the weather data collection to have students think about when to use samples to predict.
2. Tie in the Adventure Book *It's Sunny in Arizona* with this lab.

Connection

Read and discuss *Weather Forecasting* by Gail Gibbons.

Answer Key is on pages 89–93.

Notes:

Weekend Weather

Dear Family Member:

Throughout the month, your child will observe and record sky conditions as part of a study of weather. (You might recall that we collected similar data earlier in the year.) In order to have complete information, we ask you to help your child record the weekend skies. It is important that the observation be made as close to the indicated time as possible.

Time of Day: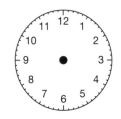

On Saturday, it was:

On Sunday, it was:

Be ready to report the weekend weather on Monday.

Blackline Master

Student Guide (p. 227)

Weather 2 Calendar

Answers will vary depending upon weather.*

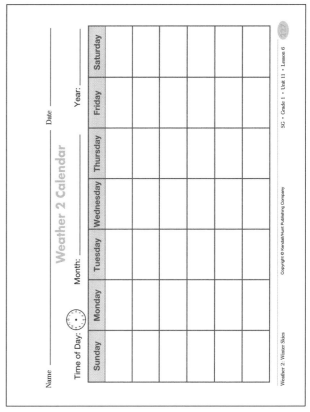

Student Guide - page 227

Student Guide (p. 229)

Weather 2 Picture

See Figure 4 in Lesson Guide 6 for a sample picture.*

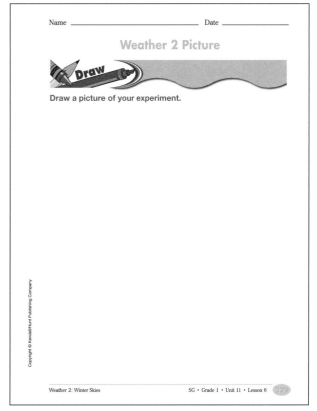

Student Guide - page 229

*Answers and/or discussion are included in the Lesson Guide.

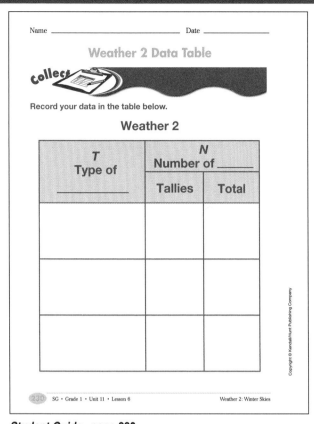

Student Guide - page 230

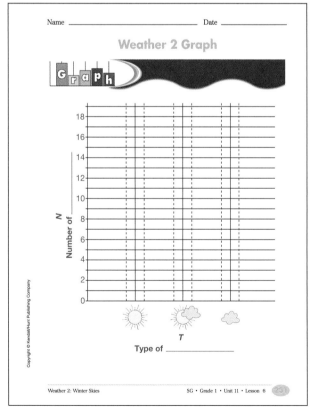

Student Guide - page 231

Student Guide (p. 230)

Weather 2 Data Table

Table will vary depending upon collected data.

Student Guide (p. 231)

Weather 2 Graph

See Figure 5 in Lesson Guide 6 for a sample graph.*

*Answers and/or discussion are included in the Lesson Guide.

Student Guide (p. 232)

Thinking about Winter Skies

Answers will vary.

Name _____ Date _____

Thinking about Winter Skies

Explore

1. Which type of sky did you see *most* often?
   _____

2. Which type of sky did you see *least* often?
   _____

3. How many sunny *and* partly sunny skies were there in all?
   _____

4. Were there more cloudy skies or more sunny skies?
   _____

5. How many days are there in half of this winter month?
   _____

6. A. Was any type of sky seen on more than half the days
   in the month? _____

   B. Which type of sky was it? _____

SG • Grade 1 • Unit 11 • Lesson 6 — Weather 2: Winter Skies

Student Guide - page 232

Student Guide (pp. 233–234)

Comparing Fall and Winter Skies

Answers will vary.*

Name _____ Date _____

Comparing Fall and Winter Skies

Explore

Record your data for each month's weather in the data table.

T Type of Sky _____	*N* Number of Days	
	month	month
☀		
🌤		
☁		

1. A. Which month had more sunny days? _____

   B. How many more? _____

   C. Is this a big difference or a small difference?
   _____

Weather 2: Winter Skies   SG • Grade 1 • Unit 11 • Lesson 6

Student Guide - page 233

Name _____ Date _____

2. A. Which month had more partly sunny days?
   _____

   B. How many more? _____

   C. Is this a big difference or a small difference?
   _____

3. A. Which month had more cloudy days? _____

   B. How many more? _____

   C. Is this a big difference or a small difference?
   _____

4. When would you expect more cloudy days—an autumn
   month or a winter month?
   _____

   How can you use the data to answer this question?
   _____
   _____
   _____

SG • Grade 1 • Unit 11 • Lesson 6   Weather 2: Winter Skies

Student Guide - page 234

*Answers and/or discussion are included in the Lesson Guide.

Student Guide - page 237

Student Guide - page 238

Student Guide (pp. 237–238)

Weather Problems*

Answers will vary.

1. 10 sunny days; $7 + 3 = 10$
2. 5 cloudy days; $9 - 4 = 5$
3. 13 cloudy days; $9 + 4 = 13$
4. $16 + 13 + 7 + 3 = 39$; yes. Solution strategies will vary.

Students' journal problems will vary.

*Answers and/or discussion are included in the Lesson Guide.

Student Guide (p. 239)

Winter Weather

B & D; stories will vary.

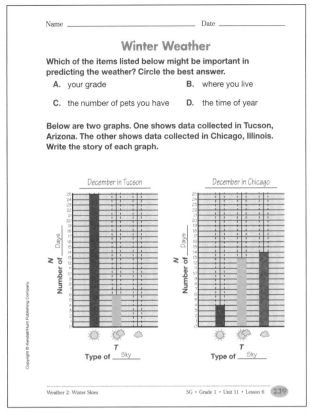

Student Guide - page 239

Unit Resource Guide (p. 88)

Weekend Weather

Answers will vary.

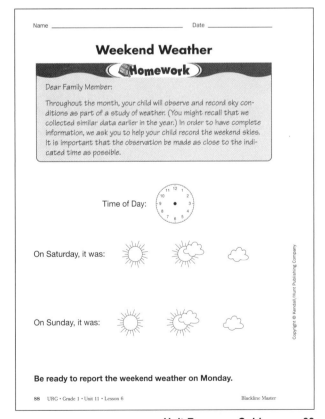

Unit Resource Guide - page 88

It's Sunny in Arizona

Lesson Overview

Estimated Class Sessions

1

This *Adventure Book* follows the January adventures of a family traveling from cloudy, cold Chicago, Illinois, to sunny, dry Tucson, Arizona. As they travel south and west, family members notice the weather changing, becoming warmer and drier.

Before presenting the *Adventure Book,* use the *U.S.A. Map* Activity Page in the *Student Guide* to discuss how to find the direction you are traveling on the map. Practice locating states and finding a state that is north, south, east, or west. While presenting the story, ask students to describe the action in each of the pictures before you read the text. Allow students time to discuss each page, and identify the geographic location of the family on the *U.S.A. Map* Activity Page.

Key Content

- Understanding that when the variable *location* is changed, weather changes might be observed.
- Finding directions on a map (north, south, east, west).
- Connecting mathematics and social studies to real-world events: using a map.

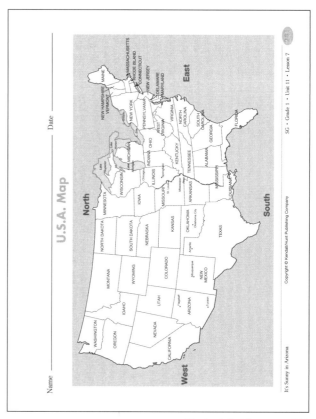

Student Guide - page 241

Materials List

Supplies and Copies

Student	Teacher
Supplies for Each Student Pair • crayons	**Supplies**
Copies	**Copies/Transparencies** • 1 transparency of *U.S.A. Map,* optional (*Student Guide* Page 241)

All blackline masters including assessment, transparency, and DPP masters are also on the Teacher Resource CD.

Student Books

U.S.A. Map (*Student Guide* Page 241)
It's Sunny in Arizona (*Adventure Book* Pages 41–56)

Daily Practice and Problems

DPP items Q–R (*Unit Resource Guide* Page 25)

Daily Practice and Problems

Suggestions for using the DPPs are on page 102.

Q. Nickels and Dimes (URG p. 25)

1. How many dimes are in 40 cents?
2. How many nickels are in 40 cents?
3. How many dimes are in 70 cents?
4. How many nickels are in 70 cents?

R. Nicky and Demi (URG p. 25)

1. Nicky has 4 nickels. How much are her coins worth?
2. Demi has 6 dimes. How much are her coins worth?
3. How much money do the two girls have altogether?

Adventure Book - page 42

Page 42

- *Describe the weather in Chicago.*

Snowy and cold

Adventure Book - page 45

Page 45

- *Locate **Chicago, Illinois,** on your map. This is where the adventure begins.*

Page 46

- *What did the family notice about the weather?*

It started to rain.

Adventure Book - page 46

Page 47

- *Point to **Springfield, Illinois,** on your map. Draw a line from Chicago, Illinois, to Springfield, Illinois. Which direction did the family travel?*

Mostly south and a little west

Adventure Book - page 47

Adventure Book - page 48

Page 48

- *Find **St. Louis, Missouri,** on your map. Draw a line from Springfield, Illinois, to St. Louis, Missouri. What direction did the family travel to go from Springfield to St. Louis?*

South and west

- *Find the **Mississippi River** on your map. Trace the river with a blue crayon. In what direction does the river go?*

South

- *What direction did the family travel to cross the Mississippi River?*

West

Adventure Book - page 49

Page 49

- *How did the family describe the weather at the arch?*

Cloudy, but warmer and sunnier than it was in Chicago.

Note: Explain to students unfamiliar with the St. Louis Gateway arch that it symbolizes St. Louis's role as the gateway or starting point through which the pioneers traveled on their way west.

- *Point to **Oklahoma City, Oklahoma,** on your map. Draw a line from St. Louis, Missouri, to Oklahoma City, Oklahoma. Which direction did the family travel between St. Louis and Oklahoma City?*

South and west

Page 50

• *What changes did the family notice in the weather outside of Oklahoma City?*

The weather was sunnier and drier.

• *Point to **Amarillo, Texas,** on your map. Draw a line from Oklahoma City, Oklahoma, to Amarillo, Texas. Which direction is Amarillo from Oklahoma City?*

West

Adventure Book - page 50

Page 52

• *Describe the weather near Amarillo.*

Pleasant and sunny

Adventure Book - page 52

Adventure Book - page 53

Adventure Book - page 54

Page 53

*Find **Albuquerque, New Mexico,** on your map. Draw a line from Amarillo, Texas, to Albuquerque, New Mexico. Which direction did the family travel?*

West

Page 54

- *Find **Flagstaff, Arizona,** on your map. Draw a line from Albuquerque, New Mexico, to Flagstaff, Arizona. Which direction did the family travel?*

West

- *How did the family describe the weather there?*

With snow but warm

Note: Children may ask how it can be warm in a place where you can see snow. Explain that in mountain areas the snow often remains at the higher altitudes while in the valleys or deserts below the weather is warm.

Page 55

- *Describe the weather near Flagstaff, Arizona.*

Warm and sunny

Adventure Book - page 55

Page 56

- *Find **Tucson, Arizona,** on your map. Draw a line from Flagstaff, Arizona, to Tucson, Arizona. Which direction did the family travel?*

South

Adventure Book - page 56

DPP items Q and R practice finding the value of a collection of coins.

- After students finish the story, pose the following problem to the class: *The trip from Chicago to Tucson took three days. Suppose the family traveled about the same distance each day. Work with your partner to locate where the family stopped each night. Use your map, the route you marked, and a string as tools to help you solve the problem. Draw an X to show where the family stopped each night.*

- Invite partners to share their solutions with the class.

Lesson 8

Maria's Marble Mart

Lesson Overview

For many students, counting by tens, adding tens, and subtracting tens are an extension of corresponding work with ones. Similarly, there is a connection between counting on or back by ones and counting on or back by tens. This activity extends students' addition and subtraction knowledge to adding and subtracting multiples of ten as they create and solve addition and subtraction problems by counting by tens. Each problem can be solved in several ways.

Key Content

- Solving addition and subtraction problems using multiples of ten.
- Writing number sentences for addition and subtraction situations.
- Counting by tens.
- Finding several solutions for the same problem.
- Communicating solutions orally and in writing.

Math Facts Strategies

DPP item T provides math facts practice.

Assessment

1. Use the *Marble Orders* Activity Page, Assessment Indicator A2, and the *Observational Assessment Record* to document students' abilities to solve addition problems using multiples of ten.
2. Use the Journal Prompt to assess students' abilities to solve addition problems and describe solution strategies.
3. Transfer appropriate documentation from the *Observational Assessment Record* for Unit 11 to *Individual Assessment Record Sheets*.

Materials List

Supplies and Copies

Student	Teacher
Supplies for Each Student Pair • 6 index cards • 80–100 connecting cubes	**Supplies** • 10 trains of connecting cubes, each containing 10 cubes
Copies	**Copies/Transparencies** • 1 transparency of *Maria's Marble Mart* (*Student Guide* Page 242) • 1 transparency of *Marble Orders,* optional (*Student Guide* Page 243)

All blackline masters including assessment, transparency, and DPP masters are also on the Teacher Resource CD.

Student Books
Maria's Marble Mart (*Student Guide* Page 242)
Marble Orders (*Student Guide* Page 243)

Daily Practice and Problems
DPP items S–V (*Unit Resource Guide* Pages 26–27)

Assessment Tools
Observational Assessment Record (*Unit Resource Guide* Pages 13–14)
Individual Assessment Record Sheet (*Teacher Implementation Guide,* Assessment section)

Daily Practice and Problems

Suggestions for using the DPPs are on page 108.

S. Sally and Tommy (URG p. 26)

Sally Square is 3 inches by 3 inches. Tommy Triangle is $4\frac{1}{2}$ square inches. Which shape has the greater area?

T. What's the Weather Like? (URG p. 26)

1. In Chicago last week, 5 days were sunny and 2 days were cloudy. How many more days were sunny?
2. In Seattle last week, 6 days were cloudy and 1 day was sunny. How many more days were cloudy than sunny?

U. *Arrow Dynamics* (URG p. 27)

Troy was on 79.

He spun ↓ (+ 10) and then ⟶ (+ 1).

Where did he land?

Alex was on 68.

He spun ↓ (+ 10) and then ↓ (+ 10).

Where did he land?

1. Write a number sentence for Troy's moves and another for Alex's moves.
2. Who is winning?

V. Numbers (URG p. 27)

1. What number is two more than 11?
2. What number is three less than 7?
3. What number is one more than 19?
4. Name an even number between 4 and 10.
5. Name an even number between 10 and 15.

Student Guide - page 242

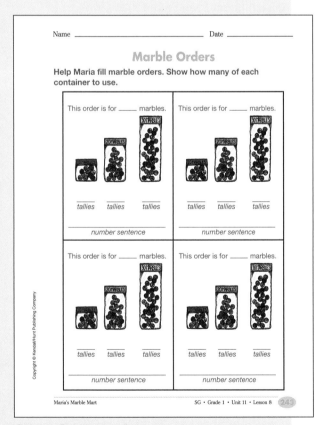

Student Guide - page 243 *(Answers on p. 111)*

Make a set of six index cards for each student pair. Write one of the following numbers on each card: 40, 50, 60, 70, 80, and 90.

Teaching the Activity

Part 1 **Addition**

Display ten trains of ten connecting cubes and ask students to count them by tens with you. Then, put three trains together so that you have a single train of 30 cubes. Tell students that you are adding two more tens as you join two other trains to the 30 cubes. Ask them to count along with you: 30, 40, 50. You can repeat this scenario with other examples.

Displaying a transparency of the *Maria's Marble Mart* Activity Page on the overhead, tell the following story:

> *Maria owns a marble store. When she opened her latest shipment of marbles from the warehouse, she was surprised. Some of the sealed bags contained 10 marbles, some had 20, and some had 30. None of the bags contained 40, 50, or 60 marbles. Now Maria has a real problem: How is she going to fill orders for more than 30 marbles? She needs our help to fill her customers' orders.*

Quickly sketch the order form on the board (or use a transparency of the *Marble Orders* Activity Page). Tell students that Maria's first order is for 50 marbles and ask how she can fill the order. As students share ways of obtaining 50 marbles using the bags of 10, 20, and 30 marbles, make tally marks showing the number of each kind of bag and write the number sentence.

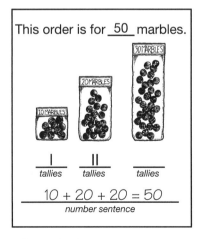

Figure 6: *One completed order form for the order of 50 marbles*

A volunteer can verify each solution by using the stacks of connecting cubes. Encourage students to find as many solutions as they can.

Using the *Marble Orders* Activity Page, students can help Maria fill her marble orders. Each pair should mix up their index cards with the numbers 40, 50, 60, 70, 80, and 90 and place the cards face down. Each card represents a customer's order for a specific quantity of marbles. To begin, they will draw one card and write this number at the top of an order slip. Then, they use tally marks to show one way to fill the order. An order slip is completed by writing a number sentence showing the bags and the order total at the bottom. Each pair should complete four different customer orders.

After the activity, have the class help you list the various ways to find each customer order. Here are some examples for an order of 50 marbles:

- $10 + 20 + 20 = 50$
- $30 + 20 = 50$
- $10 + 30 + 10 = 50$
- $20 + 10 + 10 + 10 = 50$
- $10 + 10 + 10 + 10 + 10 = 50$

Journal Prompt

Erika filled an order using a bag of 30 marbles and a bag of 20 marbles. Write a number sentence for this marble order. Explain the strategy you used to add.

Part 2 Subtraction

Show the transparency of *Maria's Marble Mart* and discuss how, in the first part of the lesson, students helped Maria fill orders by combining packages of 10, 20, and 30 marbles. Tell students that Maria now gets marbles packaged only in bags of ten. Ask students to count by tens to 100.

Let students know that they are going to solve problems about selling bags of marbles packaged in tens. In these problems, we need to know how many marbles Maria has when she starts and how many she sells. With this information, students will find out how many marbles she has left. Have students solve the following problem:

Maria had 50 red marbles. She sold 40 of them. How many red marbles did Maria have left to sell? (10)

After they solve the problem, ask students to share their strategies. Here are some possibilities:

- *A student counts from 40 to 50 by tens: "40, 50."*
- *A student shows five stacks of ten cubes and takes away four stacks.*
- *A student shows five stacks of ten cubes and covers up four stacks.*
- *A student draws a picture of the situation.*

Write number sentences to represent the different combinations. When appropriate, try to connect the problem situations to subtraction number sentences.

Have pairs of students each make up one problem involving selling Maria's marbles that the rest of the class can solve. Encourage students to describe subtraction situations. (The presenting pair, in the role of the teacher, must know the answer.) Students share various ways of solving each problem.

Number sentences for the problems and their solutions may be recorded on easel paper as they are solved.

It is a natural extension to introduce multistep problems and other problem types, such as those shown here.

1. Maria's helper, Tony, had 70 red marbles in seven bags. He sold 40 marbles. Then, he found 20 more marbles in a box. How many marbles does he have now? Answer: $70 - 40 + 20 = 50$

2. Maria had 100 green marbles in ten bags. She sold 50 green marbles to Martina. Then, she sold 20 more green marbles. How many does she have left? Answer: $100 - 50 - 20 = 30$

3. Tony had 60 yellow marbles. He sold some of them, but forgot how many. Later, he noticed he had 40 yellow marbles. How many yellow marbles did he sell? Answer: $60 - 40 = 20$

4. One day, Maria sold 40 blue marbles. At the end of the day, she had 20 blue marbles left. How many blue marbles did she have when the day began? Answer: $40 + 20 = 60$

5. After lunch, Tony sold 60 marbles, and Maria sold 40 marbles. How many more marbles did Tony sell than Maria? Answer: $60 - 40 = 20$

Math Facts Strategies

DPP item T provides practice with the subtraction math facts in the context of weather.

Homework and Practice

DPP item S provides practice measuring and comparing areas of shapes. Item U reviews using the *100 Chart* in the *Arrow Dynamics* game. Item V develops number sense for small numbers.

- Use the *Marble Orders* Activity Page and the *Observational Assessment Record* to document students' abilities to solve addition problems using multiples of ten.
- Use the Journal Prompt to assess students' abilities to solve addition problems and describe solution strategies.
- Transfer appropriate documentation from the *Observational Assessment Record* for Unit 11 to *Individual Assessment Record Sheets.*

Extension

Ask students to find many ways to fill an order for 100 marbles. Students can make up problems about orders that result in 100.

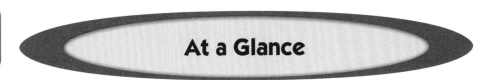

Estimated Class Sessions

2

At a Glance

Math Facts Strategies and Daily Practice and Problems

DPP item S reviews area. Item T practices math facts. Items U and V develop number sense.

Part 1. Addition   **A4**

1. Write 40, 50, 60, 70, 80, and 90 on index cards for each group of students.
2. Students skip count to add 20 cubes to 30 cubes.
3. Tell the *Maria's Marble Mart* story while displaying the transparency.
4. Students tell ways Maria could fill an order for 50 marbles.
5. Students use their index cards to fill different orders.
6. Discuss different possible ways to fill certain orders.

Part 2. Subtraction

1. Students count by tens to 100.
2. Students solve a subtraction problem and tell their strategies about selling bags of marbles packaged in tens.
3. Student pairs make up problems and challenge their peers to solve them.
4. Students solve each other's problems and write number sentences.
5. Students try multistep problems.

Assessment

1. Use the *Marble Orders* Activity Page, Assessment Indicator A2, and the *Observational Assessment Record* to document students' abilities to solve addition problems using multiples of ten.
2. Use the Journal Prompt to assess students' abilities to solve addition problems and describe solution strategies.
3. Transfer appropriate documentation from the *Observational Assessment Record* for Unit 11 to *Individual Assessment Record Sheets.*

Extension

Have students find many ways to fill an order for 100 marbles.

Answer Key is on page 111.

Notes:

Student Guide (p. 243)

Marble Orders

Answers will vary depending upon the number of marbles ordered. See Figure 6 for a sample order of marbles.*

Name _____ Date _____

Marble Orders

Help Maria fill marble orders. Show how many of each container to use.

This order is for ____ marbles.

_____ _____ _____
tallies tallies tallies

_____
number sentence

This order is for ____ marbles.

_____ _____ _____
tallies tallies tallies

_____
number sentence

This order is for ____ marbles.

_____ _____ _____
tallies tallies tallies

_____
number sentence

This order is for ____ marbles.

_____ _____ _____
tallies tallies tallies

_____
number sentence

Maria's Marble Mart

SG • Grade 1 • Unit 11 • Lesson 8

Student Guide - page 243

*Answers and/or discussion are included in the Lesson Guide.

Glossary

This glossary provides definitions of key vocabulary terms in the Grade 1 lessons. Locations of key vocabulary terms in the curriculum are included with each definition. Components Key: URG = *Unit Resource Guide* and SG = *Student Guide.*

A

Approximate (URG Unit 12)
1. (adjective) a number that is close to the desired number
2. (verb) to estimate

Area (URG Unit 10; SG Unit 12)
The amount of space that a shape covers. Area is measured in square units.

B

C

Capacity (URG Unit 9)
1. The volume of the inside of a container.
2. The largest volume a container can hold.

Circle (URG Unit 2)
A curve that is made up of all the points that are the same distance from one point, the center.

Circumference (URG Unit 15)
The distance around a circle.

Coordinates (URG Unit 19)
(In the plane) Two numbers that specify the location of a point on a flat surface relative to a reference point called the origin. The two numbers are the distances from the point to two perpendicular lines called axes.

Counting All (URG Unit 1)
A strategy for adding in which students start at one and count until the total is reached.

Counting Back (URG Unit 8)
A method of subtraction that involves counting from the larger number to the smaller one. For example, to find 8 − 5 the student counts 7, 6, 5 which is 3 less.

Counting On (URG Unit 1 & Unit 4)
A strategy for adding two numbers in which students start with one of the numbers and then count until the total is reached. For example, to count 6 + 3, begin with 6 and count three more, 7, 8, 9.

Counting Up (URG Unit 8)
A method of subtraction that involves counting from the smaller number to the larger one. For example, to find 8 − 5 the student counts 6, 7, 8 which is 3 more.

Cube (URG Unit 12 & Unit 15)
A solid with six congruent square faces.

Cubic Units (URG Unit 12)
A unit for measuring volume— a cube that measures one unit along each edge. For example, cubic centimeters and cubic inches.

cubic centimeter

Cylinder (URG Unit 15)
A three-dimensional figure with two parallel congruent circles as bases (top and bottom) and a curved side that is the union of parallel lines connecting corresponding points on the circles.

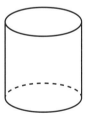 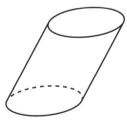

D

Data Table (URG Unit 3)
A tool for recording and organizing data on paper or on a computer.

Name	Age

Division by Measuring Out (URG Unit 14)
A type of division problem in which the number in each group is known and the unknown is the number of groups. For example, twenty students are divided into teams of four students each. How many teams are there? (20 students ÷ 4 students per team = 5 teams) This type of division is also known as measurement division.

Division by Sharing (URG Unit 14)
A type of division problem in which the number of groups is known and the unknown is the number in each group. For example, twenty students are divided into five teams. How many students are on each team? (20 students ÷ 5 teams = 4 students per team) This type of division is also known as partitive division.

E

Edge (URG Unit 15)
A line segment where two faces of a three-dimensional figure meet.

Equivalent Fractions (URG Unit 18)
Two fractions are equivalent if they represent the same part of the whole. For example, if a class has 8 boys and 8 girls, we can say $\frac{8}{16}$ of the students are girls or $\frac{1}{2}$ of the students are girls.

Even Number (URG Unit 4 & Unit 13)
Numbers that are doubles. The numbers 0, 2, 4, 6, 8, 10, etc. are even. The number 28 is even because it is 14 + 14.

F

Face (URG Unit 12 & Unit 15)
A flat side of a three-dimensional figure.

Fixed Variables (URG Unit 2, Unit 6 & Unit 11)
Variables in an experiment that are held constant or not changed. These variables are often called controlled variables.

G

H

Hexagon (URG Unit 2)
A six-sided polygon.

I

J

K

L

Length (URG Unit 6 & Unit 10)
1. The distance along a line or curve from one point to another. Distance can be measured with a ruler or tape measure.
2. The distance from one "end" to another of a two- or three-dimensional figure. For example, the length of a rectangle usually refers to the length of the longer side.

Line
A set of points that form a straight path extending infinitely in two directions.

Line Symmetry (URG Unit 7 & Unit 18)
A figure has line symmetry if it can be folded along a line so that the two halves match exactly.

Line of Symmetry (URG Unit 7 & Unit 18)
A line such that if a figure is folded along the line, then one half of the figure matches the other.

M

Making a Ten (URG Unit 13)
A strategy for adding and subtracting that takes advantage of students' knowledge of partitions of ten. For example, a student might find 8 + 4 by breaking the 4 into 2 + 2 and then using a knowledge of sums that add to ten.

$$8 + 4 =$$
$$8 + 2 + 2 =$$
$$10 + 2 = 12$$

Median (URG Unit 6 & Unit 9)
The number "in the middle" of a set of data. If there is an odd number of data, it is the number in the middle when the numbers are arranged in order. So the median of {1, 2, 14, 15, 28, 29, 30} is 15. If there is an even number of data, it is the number halfway between the two middle numbers. The median of {1, 2, 14, 15, 28, 29} is $14\frac{1}{2}$.

Mr. Origin (URG Unit 19)
A plastic figure used to help childen learn about direction and distance.

N

Near Double (URG Unit 13)
A derived addition or subtraction fact found by using doubles. For example, 3 + 4 = 7 follows from the fact that 3 + 3 = 6.

Number Sentence (URG Unit 3 & Unit 4)
A number sentence uses numbers and symbols instead of words to describe a problem. For example, a number sentence for the problem "5 birds landed on a branch. Two more birds also landed on the branch. How many birds are on the branch?" is 5 + 2 = 7.

Odd Number (URG Unit 4)
A number that is not even. The odd numbers are 1, 3, 5, 7, 9, and so on.

Origin (URG Unit 19)
A reference point for a coordinate system. If the coordinate system is a line, we can determine the location of an object on the line by the number of units it is to the right or the left of the origin.

P

Part (URG Unit 4)
One of the addends in part-part-whole addition problems.

Pattern Unit (URG Unit 7)
The portion of a pattern that is repeated. For example, AAB is the pattern unit in the pattern AABAABAAB.

Perimeter (URG Unit 6; SG Unit 12)
The distance around a two-dimensional shape.

Polygon
A closed, connected plane figure consisting of line segments, with exactly two segments meeting at each end point.

Polygons

Not Polygons

Prediction (URG Unit 5)
Using a sample to predict what is likely to occur in the population.

Prism (URG Unit 15)
A solid that has two congruent and parallel bases. The remaining faces (sides) are parallelograms. A rectangular prism has bases that are rectangles. A box is a common object that is shaped like a rectangular prism.

Q

Quadrilateral
A polygon with four sides.

R

Rectangle (URG Unit 2)
A quadrilateral with four right angles.

Rhombus (URG Unit 2)
A quadrilateral with four sides of equal length.

Rotational Symmetry (URG Unit 7)
A figure has rotational (or turn) symmetry if there is a point on the figure and a rotation of less than 360° about that point so that it "fits" on itself. For example, a square has a turn symmetry of $\frac{1}{4}$ turn (or 90°) about its center.

S

Sample (URG Unit 5)
Some of the items from a whole group.

Sphere (URG Unit 15)
A three-dimensional figure that is made up of points that are the same distance from one point, the center. A basketball is a common object shaped like a sphere.

Square (URG Unit 2)
A polygon with four equal sides and four right angles.

Symmetry (URG Unit 18)
(See Line Symmetry, Line of Symmetry, and Rotational Symmetry.)

T

Three-dimensional Shapes (URG Unit 15)
A figure in space that has length, width, and height.

TIMS Laboratory Method (URG Unit 5)
A method that students use to organize experiments and investigations. It involves four components: draw, collect, graph, and explore. It is a way to help students learn about the scientific method. TIMS is an acronym for Teaching Integrated Mathematics and Science.

Trapezoid (URG Unit 2)
A quadrilateral with exactly one pair of parallel sides.

Trial (URG Unit 6)
One attempt in an experiment.

Triangle (URG Unit 2)
A polygon with three sides.

Turn Symmetry
(See Rotational Symmetry.)

U

Using Doubles (URG Unit 13)
A strategy for adding and subtracting which uses derived facts from known doubles. For example, students use 7 + 7 = 14 to find that 7 + 8 is one more or 15.

Using Ten (URG Unit 13)
A strategy for adding which uses reasoning from known facts. For example, students use 3 + 7 = 10 to find that 4 + 7 is one more or 11.

V

Variable (URG Unit 2 & Unit 11)
A variable is something that varies or changes in an experiment.

Volume (URG Unit 9 & Unit 12;
  SG Unit 12)
1. The amount of space an object takes up.
2. The amount of space inside a container.

W

Whole (URG Unit 4)
The sum in part-part-whole addition problems.

X

Y

Z